The
RESTORATION
MOVEMENT

by ENOS E. DOWLING

Study Course
for
Youth and Adults

STANDARD PUBLISHING
Cincinnati, Ohio   3140

FOREWORD

The Restoration movement is a religious movement that began about 1800, the purpose being to restore the church to its original state in doctrine, polity, and life. The standard for this restoration is the Word of God, or, more specifically, the New Testament.

From the beginning this movement has been rooted in the conviction that the restoration of the church according to this standard is possible and desirable; that it is the only way to effect genuine Christian unity; and that the unity of the church is essential to and will eventuate in the evangelization of the world. Thus the prayer of Jesus, as recorded in the seventeenth chapter of the Gospel of John, will be fulfilled.

Leaders have spoken of restoring primitive Christianity, Bible Christianity, New Testament Christianity, apostolic Christianity, gospel order. The movement has been called the Restoration movement, the Nineteenth Century Reformation, the Current Reformation; the body of people: Christians, Christian Church, Church of Christ, Disciples, Disciples of Christ, Reformers. Campbellites and Stoneites have been two of the milder epithets freely used by those not in sympathy with its principles and activities.

Analysis of the conversions recorded in the book of Acts led to the acceptance and proclamation of the following order in conversion: faith (that faith which "cometh by hearing, and hearing by 'the word of God"), repentance, confession ("Jesus is the Christ, the Son of the living God"), baptism (immersion), for-giveness of sins, gift of the Holy Spirit (Romans 10:17; Acts 16:31; 17:30; 8:37; Matthew 16:16; Acts 2:38). Further examination of the New Testament resulted in an insistence on the autonomy of the local church, each congregation being responsible for choosing its own leaders to guide in its program of worship and service. Human creeds were rejected as bonds of fellowship and tests of orthodoxy. Acceptance of the New Testament as the all-sufficient rule of faith and practice for Christians was urged upon all.

Limitations of space make it impossible to include in these studies of this important segment of American church history many important items that would be helpful in arriving at a more comprehensive knowledge and better understanding of the rise and development of this movement. Therefore, it is recommended that a copy of James DeForest Murch's *Christians Only* (Standard Publishing, 1962) be provided for the use of the teacher in preparing to teach these lessons; it will be extremely valuable for collateral or supplementary reading. Mr. Murch's analysis of developments in the Restoration movement found in Chapters 15-23 of *Christians Only* is particularly recommended for study in connection with Chapters 11, 12, and 13 of this work. If possible, a few copies of Mr. Murch's well-written and definitive history should be added to the church library and made available to the students for individual reference and study.

It is recommended that each student have a notebook in which to record basic facts relative to the history of the movement as well as additional information and insights supplied by the teacher or others during the class sessions. Information gained through individual reading and study may also be included in this notebook. In each case be sure to indicate the source of the information for future reference.

It is hoped that through these studies each student will be challenged and inspired by the faith and devotion of the early leaders in the Restoration movement and by the principles that have been advocated, and that a continuing interest will lead to further study and to the application of these principles to present-day situations, both within the movement and without.

It is also hoped that the conviction of Alexander Campbell may be shared by each teacher and student: "The ground assumed in the proposed reformation is the highest ground which can be assumed at any time or under any circumstances, and it is the only rational and lawful ground which human ingenuity and christian integrity can propose" (*Millennial Harbinger*, 1831, p. 417).

TABLE OF CONTENTS

CHAPTER 1

American Backgrounds

Reformatory movements in religion, like movements for reform in social, economic, and political life, are sensitive to the environment of which they are a part and out of which they rise.

It is often pointed out that Christianity itself began at a time when a number of factors were favorable for the rapid spread of the gospel. Philosophers had failed to answer satisfactorily the vital questions about life and its meaning, or to provide men with adequate incentives for a significant moral life. Christ answered the questions and supplied the incentives. Greek, a language suited to clear and forceful expression of thought, was in widespread use by the peoples of the Mediterranean world. While other languages were also known and used, Greek provided the common medium through which the gospel could be made known to all. A splendid network of roads facilitated communication and travel. Free access was provided to all nations, and the gospel was soon carried throughout the Roman Empire. And it was a time of peace; no major war impeded the progress of the messengers of the Prince of Peace.

Some consideration, then, of those environmental factors prevalent in America at the close of the eighteenth century—political, economic, moral, and religious—should contribute to a better understanding of the rise and development of the Restoration movement.

POLITICAL AND ECONOMIC CONDITIONS

Americans were involved in three wars during the latter part of the eighteenth century and the early years of the nineteenth. The American phase of the struggle for power between England and France in the latter half of the eighteenth century is known as the French and Indian War (1754-1763). A few years of uneasy peace and mounting tension were followed by the Revolutionary War (1775-1783). British interference with American trade, including the impressment of sailors from American ships

7

for service on British vessels, and intrigue in American political affairs, resulted in the War of 1812 (1812-1814).

The Revolutionary War was a struggle by the colonies for independence and self-determination. The defeat of the British brought political freedom to the colonies. This newfound freedom marked every phase of the development of American life, including the religious life. Those who had hazarded their lives for the sake of conscience and liberty would be little inclined to surrender either in religious matters. A rugged individualism based upon the right to worship without interference from others was to mark American Christianity. Freedom under rightful authority, an appeal to the ultimate truth as found in Jesus and the New Testament, with individual freedom in matters not revealed, was to be a basic principle of the Restoration movement.

The Louisiana Purchase in 1803 greatly enlarged the borders of the United States. The stream of immigrants from the East poured into the older sections of the West and on into this new territory. The Restoration movement accompanied this westward expansion and was so identified with it that the movement is often characterized as a frontier movement.

MORAL CONDITIONS

The era following the Revolutionary War saw the loss of moral sensitivity, resulting in the practical repudiation of moral obligations and responsibilities. Liberty too often was construed as license; debauchery was widespread. College students generally shared the temper of the times. Many of them, while preparing for places as leaders in the nation, failed to exhibit or to develop that moral integrity which is so vital to effective leadership. Drinking was common, even among the clergy.

Perhaps some of the blame may justly be laid to the influence of the British and French soldiers in America. But moral decay is always a part of the general demoralization accompanying war. Men incited to hatred against an enemy do not lose their ability to hate when the last shot has been fired. War's carnage and destruction tend to make life cheap and uncertain; and when life is so considered, men live primarily for the present, giving the physical appetites and passions priority over everything else.

Another factor that contributed to the low moral tone in the nation was the breakdown in religion. Lack of spirituality, quite often in the pulpit as well as in the pew, made the church ineffective. The skepticism that was prevalent in America, resulting from drinking at the fountains of English deism and French atheism, removed religious restraints and lessened moral stability.

RELIGIOUS CONDITIONS

Spiritual Life at a Low Ebb

It is generally conceded by historians that the period under consideration was one of the lowest eras spiritually in the history of America. We have already noted the impact of English philosophic deism and French atheism, both of which took their toll from among the members of the churches. The universities, such as Harvard and Yale, were openly atheistic. The works of Thomas Paine and Voltaire were read and their views adopted. It was difficult to find a Christian in these universities, and those who were willing to take their stand for Christ were subjected to ridicule and persecution.

Interest in religion was lagging, church membership declining. There were some, of course, who by voice and deportment manifested an abiding faith in the living Lord; but, generally speaking, vital Christianity was at a very low ebb. In fact, the religious conditions were so bad that some were convinced that the "light of the world" would soon be extinguished and the church become merely a relic of the past. Or, if this did not happen, Christianity would at least assume a comparatively unimportant and minor role in the lives of Americans. The outlook was dark indeed.

Desire for Religious Freedom

Religious freedom was closely associated with political freedom. Establishment was on its way out in the colonies. Nine states had established (state supported) churches at the beginning of the Revolutionary War: Massachusetts, New Hampshire, and Connecticut were Congregational; Maryland, New York, Virginia, North Carolina, South Carolina, and Georgia were Anglican, or Episcopal. The Anglican establishment was rejected by all these states except Virginia in the early period of the war, and Virginia followed their example in 1786. Congregational establishment was abolished in the New England states somewhat later: New Hampshire in 1817, Connecticut in 1818, and Massachusetts in 1833.

The new political freedom was not conducive to religious subjection. Even John Wesley, whose sympathies and prayers were with England during the Revolutionary War, and who lived and died a member of the Anglican Church, sent the following word

9

to the Methodist Societies in America at the time of their organization as the Methodist Episcopal Church in America at Baltimore in 1784:

> As our American brethren are now totally disentangled both from the State and from the English hierarchy, we dare not entangle them again either with one or the other. They are now at full liberty simply to follow the Scriptures and the primitive church. And we judge it best that they should stand fast in the liberty wherewith God has so strangely made them free.[1]

All was not to remain dark, however; there were some evidences of a revival of religious interest. History was about to repeat itself.

Religious Awakening

A spiritual drought near the beginning of the eighteenth century had been relieved by the period of refreshing religious revival known as the Great Awakening. It began about 1733 under the preaching of such men as Gilbert Tennant, Jonathan Edwards, and George Whitefield. It revitalized both the ministry and the church, giving great impetus to education and missions. However, the Great Awakening was followed by another period of spiritual apathy, as noted above. But the call for a return to faith in God and to a vital religious practice in harmony with this faith was again to reverberate throughout the nation.

The second religious awakening in America during the eighteenth century came during the latter part of this century. It was most pronounced in the South and West, but was not confined to these areas. The colleges had a rebirth of religious interest and commitment under the preaching and teaching of such men as Timothy Dwight, president of Yale. Dwight was an excellent preacher and an able apologist for Christianity. He refuted the arguments of the deists and atheists and called for a return to Christ and His Word.

We shall note later the development of the great camp meetings, fostered by the dramatic and soul-searching preaching of men like James McGready (Presbyterian) and the McGee brothers, John and William, one a Presbyterian and the other a Methodist. The Cane Ridge Revival, in which Barton Stone and other members of presbyteries associated with the Presbyterian Synod of Kentucky were involved, was a part of this revivalistic movement. The participation of Stone and others in these meetings was to be one factor in their trial and expulsion by presbytery and synod, although the charges against them were primarily charges of violating the doctrines set forth in the *Westminster Confession*.

10

Creeds as Religious Standards

The Protestant Reformation of the sixteenth century had promulgated the following principles: the all-sufficiency of the Bible, the priesthood of all believers, and the right and duty of private judgment. It is with the second and third principles that we are here concerned. Since each Christian is a priest (Revelation 1:6), the Bible could no longer be considered the sole property of the ecclesiastically constituted priests, such as those made by the Roman Church, to be interpreted by them for the people. As a priest, according to the New Testament, each Christian was to read and apply the Word for himself.

In practice, however, these principles were nullified by the adoption of human creeds as standards of orthodoxy and the basis for Christian fellowship. Each Christian might read and apply Biblical truths as he saw them, but he could have fellowship with others only by accepting the statement of their understanding of the Bible as incorporated in a creed. In one breath the Christian was told, "You have the right and the duty to use your own judgment in interpreting the Bible"; in the next, "If you expect to have fellowship with us your interpretation must agree with ours." Alexander Campbell caricatured this use of creeds in his "Parable of the Iron Bedstead."[2] The Restoration movement was to seek abandonment of creeds as tests of fellowship.

A Divided Church

Creeds were the seeds of sectarianism. They served as the basis for inclusion and exclusion, for unity and excommunication. They divided the church into denominational camps.

Not only were the Christian forces divided, they were also engaged in civil war. Jealousies, party spirit, striving for supremacy: these marred the peace of Zion. The broader implications of Jesus' statement found in Matthew 12:25 had been overlooked or ignored: "Every kingdom divided against itself is brought to desolation; and every city or house divided against itself shall not stand." The Restoration movement was to point out the evils of division, call for the cessation of civil war, and plead for the unity of Christian forces through a return to the Word of God as the *only* standard.

Calvinistic Theology

Calvinism was the dominant theological system in America as well as in Europe. The Methodists were Arminian, but the

Presbyterians and Baptists, from whose ranks came many of the early leaders of the Restoration movement, were Calvinistic in theology.

Calvinism is essentially the theology of Augustine carefully systematized and logically applied. Calvin's basic foundation or starting point for his doctrinal system was *the absolute sovereignty of God.* His system has been summarized in five points: total depravity, or human inability; election and predestination; limited atonement; irresistibility of grace; and perseverance of the saints. Let us look briefly at these doctrines as taught at that time.

Total Depravity. As the consequence of transgression in the Garden of Eden all the descendants of Adam became totally depraved, incapable of response to God. So deranged is the nature of man that "he could not do good if he would, and would not if he could." He must, therefore, depend *solely* upon God's grace for salvation.

Election and Predestination. God, by divine decree, chose (elected) certain individuals to salvation. Those whom He elected He predestined to eternal life; all others are predestined to eternal damnation or everlasting punishment. Some believed that this election took place before the fall; others, that it followed Adam's sin.

Limited Atonement. Christ died *only* for the elect. The blood He shed has meaning only for the chosen one. His death in no way affects the lives or destiny of the non-elect; for them there is no hope, no salvation.

Irresistibility of Grace. Election is a manifestation of the grace (unmerited favor) of God. Since He is absolute sovereign, no one can resist or reject the expression of His mercy and goodness.

Perseverance of the Saints. God's decree of election must stand. One of His elect *cannot* be lost; or, in terms familiar to us today, "once in grace always in grace."

Conversion

The doctrine of conversion was determined by this Calvinistic theology. Salvation is by faith—"only believe." But all human nature is totally depraved and incapable of any good or response to God, and no man can do anything to merit or achieve salvation, so the sinner *cannot* believe. Therefore, saving faith is imparted to the elect through the direct and miraculous operation of the Holy Spirit, and the blood of Christ cleanses from all sin. God's grace continues to provide for every need and insures the Christian's faithfulness until death, when he will receive "the crown of life" which has been secured by the election of God.

Both Calvinists and Arminians invited sinners under "conviction" to the "mourner's bench" to pray and to be prayed for. By "praying through," either at the "mourner's bench" or elsewhere, sinners received assurance that God had pardoned and accepted them. This assurance brought peace of mind and soul and great joy. It was often associated with a vision or some other "sign" from God.

To many, who were accustomed to Calvinism and the "mourner's bench" conversions, the preaching and practice of those associated in the Restoration movement must have seemed cold and mechanical. They presented a rational and Scriptural program of conversion, preaching that faith was the belief of testimony, that all men can believe, that Christ died for all men; therefore, all *may* come to Christ and all *can* turn to Him and be saved through His blood. Inquiring sinners who asked, "What shall we do to be saved?" were often answered with the words of Peter on the Day of Pentecost (Acts 2:38). Sinners were not invited to a "mourner's bench" to pray, but to a public confession of their faith, followed by baptism into Christ for the remission of sins.

Neglect and Misuse of the Bible

Nominally, the Bible was the standard for all Christians. But we have already seen that in practice the authority of the Bible was limited by the use of creeds. Thomas Campbell was judged worthy of censure and excommunication by the Seceders for holding doctrines not in harmony with the *Westminster Confession,* and a few years later his son faced charges of heresy for teaching doctrines contrary to the Baptist standard, the *Philadelphia Confession.*

In using the Bible, no distinctions were made between the Old and New Testaments, or the covenants that they represented. Both were considered binding upon Christians, the words of Moses being considered equally authoritative with the words of Christ and His apostles. Thomas Campbell, in the *Declaration and Address,* emphasized the unity of the Bible, but insisted that the New Testament is "a perfect constitution for the worship, discipline, and government of the New Testament Church." Alexander Campbell, in his *Sermon on the Law,* given before the Redstone Baptist Association in 1816, made a distinction between the law and the gospel as set forth in the Old and New Testaments.

This, he says, precipitated a "seven years' war" with the Baptists, particularly certain of the clergy.

THE CLERGY

While there were many consecrated ministers conscientiously serving God during the period under consideration, generally the "clergy" were deemed an ambitious and arrogant lot. Alexander Campbell believed the clergy to be responsible for much, if not all, that was evil, unwanted, unscriptural, and unnecessary in the church. He regarded them as "hirelings" or "hireling priests" more concerned about money than men, certain that they were one of the greatest enemies of reform. He carried on an almost incessant war against them. The early issues of the *Christian Baptist* are literally filled with castigations of the clergy. The editor's "Sermon Upon Goats"[3] and "The Third Epistle of Peter"[4] are stinging satires on the ambitions, claims, and work of the clergy.

Such, then, were the conditions in America about the beginning of the nineteenth century. It is against this background that we must see and interpret the activities of the early leaders of the Restoration movement.

Questions

1. What part does environment play in religious movements?
2. What effect did the Revolutionary War have upon the moral and religious conditions in America?
3. What political conditions in America were significant for the beginning of the Restoration movement?
4. Describe the prevalent type of religious conversion in America at the beginning of the nineteenth century.
5. What was the relative importance of the Bible and creeds as religious standards at this time?

Notes

[1]W. E. MacClenny, *Life of Rev. James O'Kelly,* p. 48.
[2]*Christian Baptist,* Burnet edition, pp. 277, 278.
[3]*Ibid.,* Vol. I, pp. 26-28. Omitted from the Burnet edition.
[4]*Ibid.,* Burnet edition, pp. 166-168.

CHAPTER 2

Contemporary Movements—I James O'Kelly, Abner Jones, Elias Smith

Nineteenth-century America provided fertile soil for the planting and growth of religious reformation. Both need and opportunity were present. Spiritual life was exceedingly low, desperately in need of renewed vitality. Long-established religious traditions and practices present in the Old World had lost much of their awesome power over the lives of men in the atmosphere of freedom which enveloped the new nation.

In the South, East, and West, almost simultaneously, movements sprang up for repudiation of ecclesiastical authority and doctrines imbedded in traditions and human creeds. These movements advocated a return to the New Testament as the all-sufficient guide for Christians. Even Great Britain was affected by similar movements. To the naturalistic interpreter of history the circumstances that occasioned and furthered these movements may seem accidental, but the student having a different philosophy of history sees in them the hand of God.

Three things should be kept in mind as we consider the contributions of the early leaders in these reformatory movements in America: (1) although living in a new country, they did not break from the established religious order without a struggle; (2) a full understanding and concise statement of restoration principles were not arrived at immediately; and (3) these leaders did not foresee the ultimate place to which their actions would bring them.

Habit, sentiment, doctrine, and personal elements are involved in such movements. There is a religious habit, that familiar religious pattern in which the Christian worships, serves, and lives; and it is as difficult to break as habits in other areas of life, probably even more difficult. The religion to which our ancestors are or have been committed acquires a certain sacredness. If living, the presence of these loved ones makes any defection from *their* religion difficult;

15

if dead, the ties may be even stronger. Doctrinal concepts have a way of remaining in the memory once they have been taught, received, and associated with religious practice. In some instances these may be modified, but it is difficult to forsake them entirely. Warm friendships and fellowship incline one to be more tolerant of differences. Only under the power of conviction too great to be denied and circumstances that can no longer be tolerated does the break finally occur.

In a sense these men "saw through a glass, darkly." It is doubtful that they foresaw the cherished doctrines that had to be abandoned if the restoration they proposed was to be consistent and meaningful. Fellowship would be completely broken or denied; they would be subjected to bitterness, misunderstanding, and misrepresentations. Thomas Campbell, for example, was slow to perceive that it was one thing to announce the slogan, "Where the Scriptures speak, we speak; where the Scriptures are silent, we are silent," and quite another to put it fully and completely into practice. Others actually saw some of its implications more clearly than Campbell. Certainly the determined opposition of the Chartiers Presbytery was not anticipated.

THE MOVEMENT IN NORTH CAROLINA AND VIRGINIA

The beginning of the movement for a return to primitive Christianity in North Carolina and Virginia is attributed largely to the influence and activities of James O'Kelly. Little is known of his birth and early life. He was probably born in 1735; he died in 1826. W. E. MacClenny, in *The Life of Rev. James O'Kelly* (1910), concludes that he was born and educated in Ireland and came to America rather early in his life, settling first in Virginia and later in North Carolina.

O'Kelly was converted by the Methodists at the age of thirty-nine and soon began laboring among them as a lay (unordained) preacher. He was not ordained until some ten years later. As a preacher he developed quite rapidly and soon became a man of influence and power, being favorably received by the people and by his fellow ministers.

Methodists in America

The Methodists in America were a part of the movement launched by John Wesley in England. This Anglican divine, repelled by the coldness and formality in the life and worship of the Church of England, became the leading spirit in a movement

16

to revitalize this body. Societies for developing genuine piety and a deeper devotional life were organized. The members followed a carefully outlined program, which included self-interrogation in religious matters, prayer, and reading the Bible and selected devotional literature. They communed frequently and visited almshouses and prisons. They were called "Methodists" because they lived by rule or method.

Methodist societies were organized in America, following the same general pattern and purposes as those in England. While the members of these societies worshiped together, they lacked ministers who were qualified by ordination to administer the ordinances of baptism and the Lord's Supper, to solemnize marriage, and to bury the dead. For these important functions ministers of the Anglican Church had to be sought out. But the people had little desire or inclination to call upon these ministers, for they were generally considered to be lacking in piety and morality, spiritually unqualified to perform such sacred tasks.

The Revolutionary War wrought havoc in the Anglican Church in America. Many of the ministers in American churches were Englishmen who forsook their people and returned to their native land. Many of those who did not go home favored and worked for the British during the war. O'Kelly served on the side of the colonies.

Following the Revolutionary War, John Wesley chose Thomas Coke and Francis Asbury to be joint superintendents of the Methodists in America. Richard Whatcoat and Thomas Vasey were ordained and sent to administer the ordinances. In 1784, at the suggestion and with the blessing of Wesley, the Methodists organized their own religious body, calling it the Methodist Episcopal Church in America. Asbury was ordained, in succession, Deacon, Elder, and Superintendent. James O'Kelly was one of thirteen ordained as Elders.

Some, however, were not satisfied with a strict episcopacy, but were unable to prevent the setting up of this type of church government. Leading the opposition was O'Kelly. He argued that a sacrifice of freedom was being demanded, a freedom as vital in religion as in the state; that there was no New Testament precedent for such an organization. Had not Mr. Wesley written the Methodists in America that they were "at full liberty simply to follow the Scriptures and the primitive church"? The system practically ignored the people and their wishes, and placed all power in the hands of the clergy.

17

"The Right of Appeal"

Asbury's autocratic demands and growing power greatly alarmed O'Kelly. Tension increased between the "Bishop" and the "Elder" as the latter continued to oppose the governmental developments in the Methodist body.

The General Conference for 1792 was held in Baltimore. Both Asbury and O'Kelly recognized the importance of this meeting and labored to have those in favor of their particular positions in readiness at the conference. It was here that O'Kelly presented his "Right of Appeal" motion in an attempt to apply some check on the power of Asbury: "After the Bishop appoints the preachers to their several circuits, if any one thinks himself injured by the appointment, he shall have the liberty to appeal to the Conference and state his objection, and if the Conference approve his objection, the Bishop shall appoint him to another circuit."

After some discussion this motion was divided into two parts: (1) should the bishop appoint the preachers to their circuits? and (2) should any preacher be allowed the right of appeal? Little or no opposition was offered to the first part, and it was accepted. Debate on the latter part, however, was prolonged, being "kept a full week upon the anvil of discussion, and was beaten out of all shape."[1] When the vote was finally taken the motion was lost.

O'Kelly may have "out-argued" his opponents, but they "out-generaled" him. He was accused of trying to "impeach the Bishop" and was otherwise placed in a bad light. The harsh and belligerent attitude of O'Kelly and his friends, proved so distasteful to many who favored his position in the beginning that they voted against O'Kelly's motion. As a result, O'Kelly and several other ministers withdrew from the conference.

The Republican Methodist Church

Those who withdrew from the conference still maintained their status as Methodists. They were permitted to preach and work among the Methodist churches wherever and whenever possible. But this proved unsatisfactory. A reconciliation was possible on the part of the O'Kellyites only by a change in the attitude of Asbury. When further discussion removed all hope of reconciliation, the O'Kelly group met in Manakintown, Virginia (1793), and organized the Republican Methodist Church. Almost a year later an "open door" conference, including laity as well as clergy, was held at the Lebanon Church, Surry County, Virginia, to consider matters relating to this religious body.

The "Republicans" Become "Christians"

Progress during the first day of this conference proved so unsatisfactory that a committee of seven was appointed to draft a plan of government for presentation to the conference. This committee also experienced difficulty in coming to an agreement. Finally, they agreed to examine the Word of God and be governed by what they found there. Rice Haggard suggested the name "Christians" (Acts 11:26) as a more suitable name for the body than "Republican Methodists." A. Hafferty, from North Carolina, moved that the Bible be recommended as their only creed. When the committee made its report, their recommendations were immediately accepted. O'Kelly writes:

The people rejoiced at the consolation, and gave glory to God for the light received. Thus the blessed *Jesus* was proclaimed *King*, and the *Head* of the people, without *one* dissenting voice, cordially renouncing all human institutions in the church, as being a species of popery, and not fit to govern souls. Then as free citizens in the land of Columbia (America), and servants of the great *King*, we proceeded according to divine order, to ordain elders.[2]

Division and Reunion

But the peace of the new Zion was soon disturbed over the proper "mode" of baptism. O'Kelly was a firm and unmovable advocate of infant baptism and sprinkling. William Guirey had become convinced that immersion was the Scriptural baptism and he and some others had been immersed. During a heated discussion of this matter, O'Kelly is said to have asked Guirey: "Who rules this body, you or I?" To which Guirey replied: "Neither of us, brother; Christ rules here."[3] As a result of this controversy the Christians divided, the immersionists continuing to use the name Christians, while the others were known as "O'Kellyites."

The immersionists organized the Virginia Christian Conference. Correspondence between representatives of this conference and the New England Christians led to a union of these two groups in 1811. This union continued until the slavery issue divided them in 1854. At this time there was a reunion of the forces of Guirey and O'Kelly. This united body of southern Christians joined with the New England group in 1890.

THE NEW ENGLAND MOVEMENT

While the movement was developing in Virginia and North Carolina, a similar movement was beginning in the New England States under the influence of Abner Jones and Elias Smith.

19

Abner Jones (1772-1841)

Abner Jones, the more stable of these two leaders, was a native of Massachusetts. He later made his home in Vermont. He was a schoolteacher, a doctor, and a preacher.

Jones led a rather dissolute and irreligious life until his conversion. He manifested an interest in religion earlier in life, but it was not until he reached the age of twenty that he was fully converted and baptized into the Baptist Church. He immediately instituted an individual study of the Bible. Within a short time he began preaching. His continued study of the Bible led him to break from the Calvinistic system held by the Baptists and to proclaim himself a Christian only. He emphasized Christian character as the only and all-sufficient test for Christian fellowship.

He was ordained by the Free Will Baptists in 1802. His preaching of the Bible had been well received by this particular group of Baptists, with whom he found himself more nearly in agreement than any other religious group. They asked Jones to affiliate with them. While he expressed a willingness to fellowship with them as Christians and to unite with them in the work of the Lord, he declared his determination to be nothing but a Christian. He wanted it clearly understood that he was not "joining" the "Free-Willers," for he would not be subject to any of their rules and regulations. He desired Christian fellowship and willingly associated with them on his own terms; that is, as long as he could remain a free man in Christ.

Among the Christian churches established by Jones were those at Lyndon, Vermont (1801); Hanover, New Hampshire (1802); Piermont, New Hampshire (1803); and Boston, Massachusetts (1804). He was associated with Elias Smith in evangelistic work for a short time.

Elias Smith (1769-1846)

Elias Smith, schoolteacher, doctor, preacher, author, and editor, was born at Lyme, Connecticut, and died at Lynn, Massachusetts. His education began at the age of four and continued in a limited way until he was thirteen. Later, according to his autobiography, he spent thirteen days in learning grammar, devoted ten days to arithmetic, and gave eight evenings to the study of music.

Smith's father was a Baptist and his mother a Congregationalist. When he was eight years old, his mother determined to have him sprinkled. The time arrived but Smith ran. He was caught and forced to submit. He manifested interest in religion at the age of five and again at sixteen. One day he slipped in the snow while carrying a log and was knocked unconscious and pinned beneath the log. When he regained consciousness, and while still held in the snow by the log, he "experienced regeneration" through the grace of God. He dated the beginning of his Christian life with this experience.

Smith found neither command nor example for infant baptism or sprinkling in the Bible, so he determined to be immersed. He was baptized into the Baptist Church. He preached his first sermon when twenty-one, and was ordained about two years later (1792). He was too restless for a located ministry, but succeeded as an evangelist.

Continued reading of the Bible made Smith dissatisfied with the Baptist doctrines. Under the influence of his brother, Uriah, he embraced Universalism for fifteen days in 1801. But he was uncertain and unsettled. He finally resolved to lay aside Calvinism and Universalism, to search and follow the Bible. By 1805 he had discarded all other books for the New Testament and was using the name Christian to the exclusion of all other names. He was an independent, an advocate of religious freedom; he refused to be a party man.

Elias Smith was rather unstable and moody at times. His religious uncertainty was to cause him great concern and lead to difficulty with the Christians. Five times he accepted and then repudiated Universalism. His Christian brethren feared to trust a man who "was blown about by every wind of doctrine."

Smith was the author of a number of religious and medical books. His editorial career began in 1805 with the publication of a quarterly entitled *The Christian's Magazine, Reviewer and Religious Intelligencer*. He later edited *The Morning Star and City Watchman* (1827-1829). Perhaps his most important contribution to the movement for a return to New Testament Christianity was the publication of the first religious newspaper in America, *The Herald of Gospel Liberty* (1808-1817). The *Herald* publicized and defended the principles of the Christians. It also served as a medium through which the Christians in the North, South, and West became acquainted with each other.

We have already noted that the southern Christians finally united with this northern group. Some of those associated with the Stone movement in Kentucky and Ohio refused to join with Stone in union with the Reformers and cast their lot with these Christians. Thus emerged the Christian Church, or the Christian denomination

21

in America. This denomination united with the Congregationalists in 1931 to form the Congregational-Christian Church. In 1957 the Congregational-Christian Church merged with the Evangelical and Reformed Church to form the United Church of Christ.

In theology the Christians were basically unitarian. Their "plea" may be outlined in six points: the Lord Jesus Christ as the head of the church; Christian the only name; the Bible as the only rule of faith and practice; individual interpretation of the Scriptures; Christian character the only test of fellowship; union of all the followers of Christ, that the world may believe.

Questions

1. Where did the Restoration movement begin in America?
2. Name three factors affecting the early leaders of the movement.
3. What was the "right of appeal"? What was its significance?
4. What church did O'Kelly organize when he left the Methodists?
5. How did this church cease and most of its members become "Christians only"?
6. What contribution did Abner Jones make to the movement?
7. What was the contribution of Elias Smith?
8. Name the six points of the "Christians."

Notes

[1]MacClenny, *Life of Rev. James O'Kelly*, p. 96.
[2]*Ibid.*, p. 117.
[3]*Ibid.*, p. 158.

CHAPTER 3

Contemporary Movements—II
B. W. Stone

A movement for return to the Bible as the only authoritative standard for Christians was inaugurated also in Kentucky near the beginning of the nineteenth century by Barton W. Stone and others. Although he was not primarily responsible for the break from Presbyterianism in which he was involved, Stone later became the acknowledged leader of the movement for reform in Kentucky and adjoining states.

Barton Stone was born near Port Tobacco, Maryland, on the day before Christmas, 1772. He died in Hannibal, Missouri, at the home of his daughter, Amanda Bowen, November 9, 1844. He was buried first in a locust grove on his farm near Jacksonville, Illinois. When the farm was sold in 1846 the body was moved to the cemetery at the Antioch Christian Church east of the city. The following year his remains were taken to Cane Ridge.

Stone has been characterized as benevolent, given to hospitality, pious, gentle, loving peace, humble, not self-seeking, fair, and yet firm in religious matters. At the time of his death A. G. Comings wrote: "I regarded him as the greatest of the Christian reformers of this century, because he was *great* as a *Christian*." Another spoke of him as "the moderator of this whole reformation."[1]

EARLY LIFE AND EDUCATION

Stone's first teacher was a firm believer in the use of the rod as an educational stimulus and perfecter of discipline. The young lad, although eager to learn, remained so frightened that he could not recite. Within a few days he was transferred to another school where he responded to kindness and developed rapidly.

The inheritance left by the father was divided by mutual agreement of all concerned when Barton Stone was sixteen. About a month after reaching the age of seventeen, young Stone entered the school of David Caldwell, which was located in North Carolina about thirty miles from his home. This school had been established some twenty-three years before. It enrolled about fifty students. Caldwell, the only teacher, was an ordained Presbyterian minister and a most thorough and competent teacher. Many graduates of his school later attained prominence in the ministry, politics, and other professions. Stone completed the classical course in 1793.

RELIGIOUS STRUGGLES

Stone's parents were members of the established church in Maryland, the Church of England. His mother later left this body and affiliated with the Methodists. Barton was sprinkled in infancy and became a member of his parents' church.

Even as a child Stone felt the need for a more vital relationship with God. He often listened to the preaching of the Baptists and Methodists. But their preaching was radically different in many respects from that of the Anglican preachers and he became confused. Years later, analyzing his religious perplexity at this period, he wrote:

My mind was much agitated, and was vascilating between these two parties. For some time I had been in the habit of retiring in secret, morning and evening, for prayer, with an earnest desire for religion; but being ignorant of what I ought to do, I became discouraged, and quit praying, and engaged in the youthful sports of the day.[2]

But Stone's religious longings were not permitted to remain dormant. The school at Guilford had been affected by the religious awakening occasioned by the fiery preaching of James McGready, a prominent Presbyterian revivalist. Many of the students had professed religion and affiliated with the Presbyterian Church. These students engaged in a period of devotions each day before morning classes. Although Stone was impressed by their piety and Christian deportment, he joined with the opposers of religion in the school. This proved unsatisfactory, however, and he became very unhappy. He had too much inborn respect for religion to be comfortable among the impious, yet was afflicted with too much uncertainty and confusion to be happy with the pious.

Stone was so unhappy and unsettled that he resolved to transfer to another school, but was prevented from doing so by "a very stormy day." He later wrote, "I remained in my room during that day, and came to the firm resolution to pursue my studies there, attend to my own business, and let every one pursue his own way."[3]

The course thus determined was not to be followed, however. He was invited by his roommate to hear James McGready again. McGready's sermon focused Stone's attention upon his perilous, unsaved condition and made him resolve to "seek first the kingdom of God and his righteousness" regardless of cost. But even then his problem was not to be easily resolved. He heard other preachers, then listened again to McGready, but failed to find what he was seeking. "For one year," he wrote later, "I was tossed on the waves of uncertainty—laboring, praying, and striving to obtain saving faith—sometimes desponding, and almost despairing of ever getting it."[4]

At last he heard a young Presbyterian preacher named William Hodge preach on the text, "God is love." What the fearful preaching of McGready could not do, the love of God revealed by Hodge accomplished. Stone read his Bible and prayed, and, finally convinced that God loved all men and that salvation was offered to all and not just the elect, he surrendered his life to God and found the peace of soul for which he had sought so long.

LICENSED BY THE ORANGE PRESBYTERY

Stone decided to give his life to the ministry. In 1793, with others from Caldwell's school, he applied to the Orange Presbytery for a license to preach. William Hodge was assigned to supervise his preparation for this event.

One of the areas of study assigned by the Presbytery was "the being and attributes of God and the Trinity." Stone was soon lost in the complexities of his problem and almost gave up his study for the ministry. Fortunately, however, a copy of Isaac Watts's *Glories of Christ* was read and the author's views accepted. The examiner appointed by the Presbytery was Henry Pattillo, who also favored Watts's explanation of this doctrine. Stone successfully passed the examination.

But he was wearied and still confused by his study of Calvinistic doctrines. Again he was almost ready to forsake his chosen work before he had really begun it. He set out for Georgia, but was taken ill on the way. He arrived at his brother Matthew's home in Georgia, where he spent some months in recovering from his illness.

Hope Hull, a Methodist preacher who had been sympathetic with O'Kelly in his battle for modification of the episcopal government as set up by the Methodists, had established a school near Washington, Georgia. He offered Stone the job of teaching languages in this institution and Stone accepted. About seventy students were enrolled. Stone proved to be a popular and successful teacher.

After a period of indecision about his future, Stone decided to fulfill his commitment to the ministry. He returned to North

Carolina to receive his license from the Orange Presbytery (1796). On this occasion he was handed a Bible by the venerable Pattillo and given this Scriptural charge: "Go ye into all the world, and preach the gospel to every creature."

Stone made a short visit with his mother in Virginia and then set out with Robert Foster to preach in the southern portion of North Carolina. His companion soon decided to give up the ministry. Stone, beset with doubts of his own fitness for the work, determined to go to Florida. He was turned from his purpose by a lady who suspected that he was "running away" and accused him of being another Jonah.

The West became the Macedonia calling for Stone's labors. He tarried for a few weeks of preaching in Virginia; then, passing through Tennessee and stopping for a short time at Knoxville and Nashville, he went into Kentucky. He soon began preaching for the Presbyterian congregations at Cane Ridge and Concord.

ORDINATION BY THE TRANSYLVANIA PRESBYTERY

Stone preached regularly for the churches at Cane Ridge and Concord as a licensed preacher. When these congregations issued a call through the Transylvania Presbytery for their preacher to locate with them, he became a candidate for ordination. An examination by the Presbytery would precede the ordination.

The standard for Presbyterians was the *Westminster Confession*, a thoroughly Calvinistic document. In his preaching Stone had carefully avoided those doctrines that had given him trouble in his early preparation for the ministry. He now faced an examination while having doubts concerning such doctrines as Trinitarianism and predestination.

October 4, 1798, was the day set for the ordination at Cane Ridge. Stone sought out two prominent members of the Presbytery, James Blythe and Robert Marshall, and explained his difficulties to them. They were unable to explain these doctrines to Stone's satisfaction. Efforts to have his ordination postponed were also unsuccessful.

During the course of the examination the candidates were asked, "Do you receive and adopt the Confession of Faith as containing the system of doctrine taught in the Bible?" To this question Stone replied in a loud voice so that all might hear, "I do, as far as I see it consistent with the word of God." No objection being offered, Stone was ordained to the Presbyterian ministry.

The mind of the newly-ordained preacher continued to be agitated by Calvinistic doctrines that he could not reconcile with reason or the Scriptures. His study of the Bible convinced Stone that God loved and desired the salvation of all; that Christ died to make this salvation possible; that the testimony in the Word was sufficient for faith; that faith would lead to repentance, and repentance to obedience. Faith and obedience would bring remission of sins, the gift of the Holy Spirit, and eternal life. Reasoning thus, Stone escaped from the "labyrinth of Calvinism and error."

THE CANE RIDGE REVIVAL

Kentucky shared in the religious revival that swept the nation at the close of the eighteenth and beginning of the nineteenth centuries. James McGready, whom Stone heard in North Carolina while attending the school of David Caldwell, was largely responsible for bringing the revival to Kentucky. He had settled in Logan County, Kentucky, in 1796.

Oppressed by the religious unconcern, the infidelity and dissipation of the people, this revivalist set aside one day of each month for fasting and prayer and an hour weekly in which to beseech God for a revival of religion and plead for the souls of men. Associated with McGready in revival efforts were the McGee brothers: William, a Presbyterian, and John, a Methodist.

Stone was also oppressed by the lack of spirituality and interest in religion by members of his congregations and those in the surrounding community. Hearing of the revival which had "broken out" in Logan County, Stone resolved to visit one of the camp meetings in the spring of 1801. He was greatly impressed by what he saw. Although many were repelled by the "religious exercises" associated with these meetings, Stone felt them to be the work of God. He returned to preach with new earnestness and enthusiasm.

The preaching of Stone at Cane Ridge and Concord were increasingly attended with manifestations of the same "religious exercises" as witnessed in Logan County. A meeting at Concord drew a large multitude of people. It lasted five days. Announcements were made for a meeting at Cane Ridge, probably during the first part of August, although opinions differ as to the exact date.

The number present at this memorable meeting has been variously estimated at ten to thirty thousand. Methodists, Baptists, and Presbyterians joined together in this revival, temporarily ignoring the doctrinal standards that divided them into opposing forces in a religious civil war.

A description and discussion of the "religious exercises" manifested in the Cane Ridge revival may be found in Part I, Chapter VI, and Part II, Chapter VI of Roger's biography of Stone. These "exercises" included falling, jerks, dancing, barking, running, laughing, and singing. The number affected was estimated from three hundred to as many as three thousand. While others have explained these as emotional or psychological phenomena, Stone believed them to be the work of God, although not necessary complements to the preaching of the gospel and conversion.

The most common was the "falling exercise," which affected both the converted and the unconverted. Some lay for as long as an hour or more in what appeared to be almost a lifeless state. When they "came to" they praised God, told of their wonderful experiences while unconscious, and exhorted sinners to repent and forsake their wicked ways.

The "jerks" also affected both saints and sinners. There was an exceedingly rapid backward and forward motion of the head or of the entire body when seized by the "jerks." The saved afterward spoke of their great ecstasy and exhilaration during the period of this "exercise," but the wicked often cursed the agitation to which they had been subjected.

Among professing Christians, and only among such, a season of the "jerks" frequently was a prelude to the "dancing exercise." Stone gives the following description of this "exercise":

Such dancing was indeed heavenly to the spectators; there was nothing in it like levity, nor calculated to excite levity in the beholders. The smile of heaven shone on the countenance of the subject, and assimilated to angels appeared the whole person. Sometimes the motion was quick and sometimes slow. Thus they continued to move forward and backward in the same track or alley till nature seemed exhausted, and they would fall prostrate on the floor or earth, unless caught by those standing by. While thus exercised, I have heard their solemn praises and prayers ascending to God.[5]

Stone associated the "barking exercise" with the "jerks," and did not consider it a genuine religious "exercise" at all. A Presbyterian preacher subjected to the "jerks" seized a sapling to prevent him from falling. As his head was jerked rapidly back and forth he emitted a noise somewhat like a bark. Someone reported that he was "barking up a tree."

The "laughing exercise" was prevalent among the religious. Instead of inducing laughter in others, it was attended with great solemnity.

The "singing exercise" was not ordinary singing. In the words of Stone:

The subject in a very happy state of mind would sing most melodiously, not from the mouth or nose, but entirely in the breast, the sounds issuing thence. Such music silenced everything and attracted the attention of all. It was most heavenly. None could ever be tired of hearing it.[6]

Judgments differed as to the significance of the Cane Ridge revival and, in fact, the whole revivalistic movement. Some saw the working of Satan; others, a marvelous outpouring of the Spirit and power of God. Some saw fanaticism and disorder; others, a miraculous transformation of lives. The revivalists themselves laid aside their denominational differences to lift a united voice in proclaiming the love and mercy of God for the penitent sinner.

JURISDICTION OF THE SYNOD OF KENTUCKY RENOUNCED

Many Presbyterian preachers were alarmed by what they saw and heard. Revivals, such as the Cane Ridge revival, were opposed for at least three reasons. The "religious exercises" so evident in the camp meetings were repugnant, violating good religious taste and order. The Presbyterian preachers were associating with uneducated and uncouth Baptist and Methodist ministers lacking proper ordination. And the *Westminster Confession* was being flouted: its doctrine of election was set aside and an invitation extended to all to come to Christ; the death of Christ for *all* and not just the elect was proclaimed; and the *ability* and *responsibility* of each individual to believe and obey the gospel was emphasized.

The attitude and activities of the Presbyterian ministers who opposed the revival and their brethren who participated in it touched off a war between Presbyterians, Methodists, and Baptists. "The spirit of partyism soon expelled the spirit of love and union—peace fled before discord and strife, and religion was stifled and banished in the unhallowed struggle for pre-eminence."[7]

Trouble was also brewing within the Presbyterian ranks. Among the Presbyterian preachers associated with the revivalistic movement in Kentucky were Barton Stone and Robert Marshall of the West Lexington Presbytery, and Richard McNemar, John Dunlavy, and John Thompson of the Washington Presbytery. The "orthodox" were determined that the revivalists' heresies in doctrine and practice should not go unnoticed; they must be rebuked and disciplined.

Attention was first focused on Richard McNemar at a special session of the Washington Presbytery, which was held in November, 1801, at Springfield, Ohio, to ordain John Thompson. (This town is not to be confused with the present Springfield. It was located about eleven miles north of Cincinnati.) A letter of complaint in six points, signed by three elders of the Cabin Creek Church, was presented at this meeting. McNemar was charged with holding and preaching doctrines contrary to the Bible and the *Westminster*

Confession, doctrines Arminian in character rather than Calvinistic. No official action was taken since a quorum was not present. By shrewd planning, his opponents succeeded in having a condemnation of McNemar entered on the minutes at the next regular meeting of the Presbytery at Cincinnati in October, 1802. In spite of this condemnation, however, McNemar was returned to Turtle Creek as pastor. At the next meeting of the Presbytery—Springfield, April, 1803—charges were made against McNemar and John Thompson. The revival men were in the majority and their opponents were voted down.

The larger Presbyterian body, the Synod of Kentucky, met at Lexington in September, 1803. Twenty-three preachers and eighteen elders were present. The committee examining the minutes of the Washington Presbytery censured the Presbytery for their handling of the charges against McNemar and Thompson, and especially for permitting McNemar to continue preaching while under condemnation. The Synod voted to sustain the action of the Presbytery against McNemar at Cincinnati.

The revivalists clearly saw that any action against McNemar would eventually be extended to them. So Stone, Dunlavy, Marshall, Thompson, and McNemar presented a statement protesting the decisions concerning McNemar and Thompson and declining all further jurisdiction of the synod. Attempts by the synod to reconcile and restore these men failed; so they were suspended, their churches declared vacant, and messengers sent to the churches with letters explaining the synod's action. Some time later they were deposed from the ministry and cut off from the Presbyterian body.

Following their renunciation of the jurisdiction of the synod, Marshall, Stone, Thompson, McNemar, and Dunlavy organized their own presbytery, calling it the Springfield Presbytery. In January, 1804, they issued *An Apology for Renouncing the Jurisdiction of the Synod of Kentucky*. Marshall, Stone, and Thompson each wrote a section. The document contains the revivalists' version of the separation from the synod, objections against making the *Westminster Confession* a standard of orthodoxy and fellowship, repudiation of the authority of all human creeds, and the all-sufficiency of the Bible as a rule of faith and practice for all Christians.

LAST WILL AND TESTAMENT OF THE SPRINGFIELD PRESBYTERY

In spite of strong opposition this new presbytery grew rapidly and soon numbered fifteen churches. Having repudiated the right of human creeds to govern in religious matters, they were led to question the place of such organized bodies as presbyteries in the church. Within a few months—June 28, 1804—*The Last Will and Testament of the Springfield Presbytery* was given to the public. It was signed by Stone, Marshall, Thompson, McNemar, Dunlavy, and David Purviance. Authorship of this document is usually attributed to Stone, but some believe that McNemar was responsible for it.

The Last Will and Testament is probably the most unusual document produced by the Restoration movement. It may be analyzed as proclamation, propaganda, and plea. It *proclaims* the dissolution of the Springfield Presbytery as an unscriptural body and inclined to produce a party spirit. It is a cleverly and carefully arranged piece of *propaganda* against the validity of human creeds as tests of fellowship and authoritative religious organizations outside the local congregation. It is a *plea* for Christians to forsake all human standards and to hold the Bible alone as the standard for faith and conduct, to practice mutual forbearance and love, and to work for the unity of the people of God.

Of the six men who signed the *Last Will and Testament*, only Stone and Purviance remained faithful to the principles set forth in the historic document. In 1805 Shaker missionaries from New York made converts of McNemar and Dunlavy. In 1811 Marshall and Thompson returned to the Presbyterians.

CHRISTIANS ONLY

The Kentucky reformers were often referred to as "Marshallites" and "Stoneites." They were also called "Newlights." In the final choice of a name they were influenced by Rice Haggard, who had been responsible for the adoption of the name Christian by the O'Kelly group in North Carolina and Virginia. Haggard suggested the use of the name Christian by this group, and for a second time his suggestion bore fruit; they became "Christians only," committed to following the Bible only.

In 1807 continued study of the divine standard led to the practice of immersion for the remission of sins. Although it was not made a test of fellowship, within a short time immersion became the common practice of the Christians in Kentucky, and their congregations were composed almost entirely of immersed believers.

Stone made an important contribution to the rise and early development of the Christians in Kentucky. His periodical, *The Christian Messenger* (1826-1845), was to be a significant force in later years.

The stone shaft marking Stone's final resting place at Cane Ridge bears this inscription: "The Church of Christ at Caneridge & other generous friends in Kentucky, have caused this monument to be erected as a tribute of affection & gratitude to BARTON W. STONE, Minister of the gospel of Christ and the distinguished reformer of the 19. Century."

Questions

1. Outline B. W. Stone's struggle in becoming a Christian.
2. What question was asked Stone at his ordination and what was his answer?
3. What was the Cane Ridge revival?
4. Describe some of the "religious exercises" associated with the Cane Ridge revival.
5. What significance did the Cane Ridge revival have for Stone and his co-laborers?
6. What was the Springfield Presbytery?
7. Who signed *The Last Will and Testament of the Springfield Presbytery*? What reasons did they give for dissolving this presbytery?
8. Describe the later actions of the six men who signed this document.

Notes

[1]Cf. John Rogers, *Biography of Eld. Barton Warren Stone,* Chapter III.
[2]Rogers, *Biography of Eld. Barton Warren Stone,* pp. 5, 6.
[3]*Ibid.,* p. 7.
[4]*Ibid.,* p. 9.
[5]*Ibid.,* p. 40.
[6]*Ibid.,* pp. 41, 42.
[7]*Ibid.,* p. 46.

CHAPTER 4

The Campbell Movement
Thomas Campbell

The Restoration movement in America is indebted to the Old Light Anti-Burgher Seceder Presbyterians in Ireland for its creative personality, Thomas Campbell. He was born in County Down, Ireland, February 1, 1763. His father, Archibald Campbell, served with the British army and participated in the capture of Quebec. A member of the Roman Catholic Church in his early life, he returned to Great Britain after the war to renounce Catholicism and become a member of the Church of England. He remained a faithful member of this church until his death.

EARLY RELIGIOUS STRUGGLES

The home life maintained by Archibald Campbell and his wife manifested the parental interest in the religious welfare of their family. The Bible was read and studied daily, and a portion of it was committed to memory. The father sought to rear his family in the traditions of the Anglican Church. But the formal worship of the Church of England lacked warmth and genuine concern and desire on the part of its members to make Christianity a vital and meaningful part of life. Repelled, Thomas Campbell sought elsewhere for more complete satisfaction of his spiritual needs. He availed himself of opportunities to hear and associate with the Covenanters and Seceders.

Thomas Campbell was influenced by the Calvinistic doctrines of hereditary total depravity and election, held and taught by the Seceder Presbyterians. He longed for the peace which would come from the assurance that he was among God's elect. He prayed diligently and sought help from friends, but this assurance was slow in coming. He became greatly disturbed by his failure to reach God and God's failure to touch and transform his life. Finally, however, assurance came. In his *Memoirs of Alexander Campbell,* R. Richardson describes Thomas Campbell's distress, inner struggle, and eventual conversion as follows:

33

While in this state, and when his mental distress had reached its highest point, he was one day walking alone in the fields, when, in the midst of his prayerful anxieties and longings, he felt a divine peace suddenly diffuse itself throughout his soul, and the love of God seemed to be shed abroad in his heart as he had never realized it. His doubts, anxieties and fears were at once dissipated, as if by enchantment. He was enabled to see and to trust in the merits of a crucified Christ, and to enjoy a divine sense of reconciliation, that filled him with rapture and seemed to determine his destiny for ever. From this moment he recognized himself as consecrated to God, and thought only how he might best appropriate his time and his abilities to his service.[1]

From the time of this religious experience, which he accepted as evidence of divine favor, he resolved to give himself to the ministry. This ministry he desired to fulfill among the Seceder Presbyterians. However, his father, unhappy because of his son's apparent change of religious affections, insisted that he devote his talents to a ministry among the Anglicans. The son was under age at the time of this conflict with his father and subject to his father's authority. Temporarily prevented from pursuing his own course by the attitude of his father, Thomas postponed a final decision.

Meanwhile, he was made aware of the need for teachers in the south of Ireland. He had received a good education in a military school near his home, so was prepared to teach. He determined to answer the call for teachers. He went to southern Ireland and established an academy in the province of Connaught. Although his teaching was greatly needed and well received, his father, still exercising his parental authority, called his son home. He soon began teaching in a school at Sheepbridge, near Newry.

John Kinley, a Seceder Presbyterian, was instrumental in obtaining this teaching appointment for Campbell. He was greatly impressed by the attitude and ability of this young teacher. Knowing of his desire to become a Seceder minister, he offered to supply the funds necessary for his ministerial education. The father, although still somewhat reluctant, finally gave his permission, and Thomas Campbell enrolled in the University of Glasgow. He pursued the three-year course prescribed for ministerial students and at the same time took advantage of the opportunity to form a limited acquaintance with the field of medicine. He desired to be able to help the poor members of his congregation who might need medical attention but were unable to afford it.

Having completed his course at Glasgow, Campbell entered the school maintained by the Anti-Burghers for further study. This school usually enrolled about twenty-five students and was taught by one man, the pastor of the church in the community where the classes were held. The course consisted of five annual sessions of eight weeks each, or an academic year of specialized study devoted to lectures and examinations in systematic theology and the *Confession of Faith*. Practical problems faced by the minister in his work were also discussed.

Campbell completed the required course of study, passed the final examinations, and was licensed as a "probationer" by the Seceder Presbyterians. He was authorized to preach the gospel in needy fields, under the supervision of the synod.

MINISTRY IN IRELAND

Thomas Campbell and Jane Corneigle were married in 1787. Mrs. Campbell was a descendant of the French Huguenots who had located in the area of Ballymena, Ireland, when they fled from France because of persecution. In 1798 the husband became the pastor of the church at Ahorey and settled with his family on a farm near Rich Hill and Newry. He also conducted an academy in order to supplement his income and provide for the needs of his family.

The new minister was welcomed because of his ability and his dedication to his work. He placed great emphasis upon the Bible in his preaching, in teaching the people of the congregation, and in his own family circle. Catechetical examinations of the children in his parish were based largely on the Bible and couched in Biblical terms rather than the words and phrases of the catechism assigned for this purpose.

As already noted, Thomas Campbell was a member of the Old Light Anti-Burgher Seceder Presbyterian Church. Presbyterianism was the established religion in Scotland. Because of efforts to enforce a law denying congregations the privilege of choosing their own ministers, in 1733 four preachers, led by Alexander Erskine, seceded from the Church of Scotland and formed the Associate Presbytery. This group was known as Seceders or the Secession Church. In 1747 the Seceders divided into Burghers and Anti-Burghers over the taking of certain oaths required of burgesses. Both the Burghers and the Anti-Burghers later divided into New Lights and Old Lights. The dispute was over the power of civil magistrates in religious affairs and the perpetuity of the *Solemn League and Covenant*, which was an agreement between the English and Scottish Parliaments. The Scots agreed to assist the English Parliament in the war against Charles I, and in return Presbyterianism was to be introduced into England and Ireland.

This divided Presbyterianism had been transplanted into Ireland. Thomas Campbell was oppressed by these useless and senseless divisions. Some of the matters responsible for divisions in Scotland were never issues in Ireland. He attempted to bring about a reunion of the Seceder Presbyterian forces. Many were sympathetic with his efforts, and he was permitted to present his proposals for union at a meeting of the Synod of Belfast. Sentiment for union grew, but the General Associate Synod of Scotland opposed the union and was able to block it for a time. However, the union for which Campbell pleaded in 1805 was finally consummated in 1820, after he had left Ireland.

EMIGRATES TO AMERICA

Thomas Campbell's labors as minister of the church at Ahorey, his teaching in the academy at Rich Hill, and his efforts to effect a reunion of the Seceders combined to break his health. Upon the recommendation of his physician, and probably in keeping with desires expressed in the family circles (his son, Alexander, had indicated a desire to go to America some day) he set sail for America in April, 1807, and arrived in Philadelphia some five weeks later.

The young Seceder preacher found the Associate Synod of North America in session upon his arrival. This synod was a Seceder ecclesiastical body; actually, it was Anti-Burgher, for the Burghers had not organized a separate body in America. The credentials which had been issued by the Presbytery at Market Hill were presented to this body, examined, and accepted. Campbell was received into the synod and assigned to labor in the bounds of the Chartiers Presbytery in southwestern Pennsylvania. This presbytery, meeting on June 30 and July 1, gave the new member appointments through October in Allegheny, Beaver, Indiana, and Washington Counties.

TROUBLE IN PRESBYTERY AND SYNOD

Within five months Campbell was in trouble with the Chartiers Presbytery. At their meeting on October 27, 1807, John Anderson informed the presbytery of his failure to keep an appointment to assist Thomas Campbell in administering the Lord's Supper at Buffaloe because he had learned of statements made by him which were not in harmony with the *Westminster Confession*. William Wilson testified that he had heard Campbell make such statements. His testimony was accepted, and Anderson was excused for not keeping this appointment. A long period of controversy was thus touched off between this preacher from Ireland and the Chartiers Presbytery.

Campbell Suspended From Presbytery

A committee consisting of four preachers (John Anderson, William Wilson, Thomas Allison, James Ramsay) and a ruling elder (John Hay) was appointed to investigate the reports made to the presbytery and to bring a libel suit against Campbell if the evidence justified it. Wilson, Allison, and Ramsay were former students of Anderson. Verbal protests and a formal letter of protest by the accused were rejected by the presbytery, and he was given no preaching appointments during November and December pending the committee's investigation.

The Chartiers Presbytery met again in January, 1808. A libel charge in several counts was presented by the committee. Campbell was charged with false teaching concerning the nature of saving faith; rejecting creeds as lawful terms of fellowship; urging ruling elders to pray and exhort in public meetings when no minister was present; that it was permissible for Seceders to hear ministers of other communions when there were no services in their own churches; repudiating the substitutionary concept of the atonement; that it is possible for one to live a sinless life; and preaching in congregations assigned to other ministers.

The libel was read and discussed item by item. Campbell was heard on each point. A copy of the libel was given to the accused, and further discussion was delayed until the next meeting of the presbytery. At the next meeting Campbell sought to defend himself against the charges, but was judged guilty on practically every count. The presbytery voted his suspension on February 12, 1808. His request for reconsideration of his case at the March meeting was voted down. After the presbytery had adjourned and many had gone home, it was again called into session with only three members present (Anderson, Wilson, and Allison), and the suspension of Campbell was made permanent.

Appeals to Synod

He appealed his case to the Associate Synod of North America. Minutes of the synod reveal that the case was discussed on May 19-21 and 23-27. The synod declared the procedure of the presbytery irregular in certain particulars and revoked their suspension. They then proceeded to their own investigation of the case. A committee instructed to make a draft of the synod's judgment concluded their report as follows:

Upon the whole, the committee are of opinion that Mr. Campbell's answer to the two first articles of charge, are so evasive and unsatisfactory, and highly equivocal upon great and important articles of revealed religion, as to give ground to conclude that he has expressed sentiments very different upon these articles, and from the sentiments held and professed by this Church, and are sufficient grounds to infer censure.[2]

Motion was made and carried to "rebuke and admonish" Campbell. A motion to reduce the sentence to admonition only was lost. Campbell then asked a delay in the execution of the judgment until the following day, and his request was granted. At the evening session he filed a protest against the judgment of the synod, stating his unwillingness to submit to censure on the grounds that his answers were "evasive, unsatisfactory and highly equivocal." He would, however, submit to admonition on the ground of having acted imprudently.

The following day, before the discussion of his case was resumed, Campbell sent a letter accusing the synod of "partiality and injustice" and declining their authority. He was summoned before the tribunal and the new development was discussed. Campbell finally admitted that he had acted hastily and agreed to take back the letter and withdraw his charges against the synod.

Further discussion of the case resulted in striking the word "evasive" from the charges. Campbell stated "that his submission should be understood to mean no more, on his part, than an act of deference to the judgment of the court, that, by so doing, he might not give offence to his brethren by manifesting a refractory spirit."[3] Following prayer by a member of the synod, Campbell was "rebuked and admonished" by the moderator. The chastened preacher was sent to Philadelphia to preach during June and July, afterward to report to the Chartiers Presbytery for further appointments.

But the leading spirits of the Chartiers Presbytery were determined that the case should not be resolved so easily. They protested the decisions of the synod, and when Campbell returned for his appointments by the presbytery, he found that none had been made. He learned that he was neither wanted nor welcome in the presbytery, and tolerated only because of the synod's order.

Campbell Withdraws From Presbytery and Synod

Campbell was irked and disgusted by the relentless and vindictive spirit of his opponents, who sought to discredit and annoy him in every possible way. Spies were selected to observe and report on his preaching and other activities; he was subjected to misrepresentations and lies. Finally, convinced that there was no hope of reconciliation with the Seceders and that no avenue of effective service was open to him within their body, Campbell presented a statement to the presbytery on September 13, 1808, renouncing the jurisdiction of the Chartiers Presbytery and the Associate Synod of North America and declaring his withdrawal from their fellowship.

Still the Chartiers Presbytery was not satisfied. It suspended Campbell from all ministerial functions. He was repeatedly called to appear before the presbytery "to be further dealt with," but he refused to appear. In May, 1809, his case was again brought before the synod. The leaders of the presbytery were determined to have the synod reverse its condemnation of the presbytery's handling of the case before it was first brought to the attention of the synod. They charged the synod with arrogance, weakness, and folly. At one point the representatives of the presbytery, John Anderson and James Ramsay, became so abusive and intolerable that the synod refused to listen to their complaints.

Campbell Censured by Presbytery

The Chartiers Presbytery continued to summon Campbell to appear, and he continued to ignore their calls. Finally, for reasons already assigned in the suspension of Campbell and "for contumacy in not appearing to answer the citations that have been sent to him," the highest censure which the presbytery could impose was executed. The records for April 18, 1810, show their disposition of the case of the troublesome Campbell:

Accordingly the Presbytery did and hereby do depose Mr. Campbell from the office of the Holy Ministry, and from sealing ordinances for the reasons above mentioned. Agreed to send an extract of this deposition of Mr. Campbell to the Synod and to intimate it to the congregations under our inspection.

CHRISTIAN ASSOCIATION OF WASHINGTON

Thomas Campbell was not idle following his withdrawal from the presbytery and synod. He preached in groves and in the homes of the community which were opened to him. The inadequacy of creeds as a basis for Christian fellowship, the unique character and supremacy of the Bible, and the desirability and necessity for the union of Christians were emphasized in his preaching.

A group composed of Christians and non-Christians, more or less sympathetic with these principles associated with Campbell, listened to his sermons, and gave him encouragement. He made no attempt to separate these people from the churches to which they belonged; he did not propose the formation of another religious party. The group had no organization of any kind. Richardson says they "were held together by a vague sentiment of Christian union, and by the personal influence and character of Thomas Campbell."[4]

The need for a more formal type of fellowship and organization was apparent. Campbell conceived the idea for a society committed to the promotion of Biblical Christianity and Christian union. The Christian Association of Washington was organized in the home of Abraham Altars on August 17, 1809.

It was at this meeting that Thomas Campbell announced the now famous slogan which was to serve as the rule or guide in all religious matters: "Where the Scriptures speak, we speak; where the Scriptures are silent, we are silent." This principle—so simple, so clear, so concise—was to become the watchword of the Restoration movement. Richardson makes the following estimate of its importance:

It was from the moment when these significant words were uttered and accepted that the more intelligent ever afterward dated the *formal and actual commencement of the Reformation* which was subsequently carried on with so much success, and which has already produced such important changes in religious society over a large portion of the world.[5]

In theory this rule was readily accepted; it was to prove much more difficult to apply in every case. In fact, when first announced, it was pointed out that a strict application of this principle would put an end to infant baptism, a practice which even Thomas Campbell was slow to relinquish. Foreseeing the necessity for giving up doctrines and religious practices that had hallowed memories and associations, within a short period of time those unwilling to commit themselves completely to this radical religious movement dropped out.

THE DECLARATION AND ADDRESS

A committee of twenty-one was selected at the organizational meeting to join with Campbell "to determine upon the proper means to carry into effect the important ends of their Association." At the next meeting of the Association in September, 1809, a document bearing the unmistakable marks of the sentiments and genius of Thomas Campbell and entitled *Declaration and Address* was presented to the Association for approval. It was accepted and ordered to be printed.

The *Declaration and Address* set forth the *purpose, policy,* and *program* of this new religious society. It consisted of four sections: "Declaration," "Address," "Appendix," and "Postscript."

The sole purpose of the Christian Association—merely a voluntary association of individuals for religious purposes and in no sense to be considered a church—as stated in the "Declaration" was to promote "simple evangelical christianity, free from all mixture of human opinions and inventions of men." Financial commitments to be paid semiannually were to provide for the support of a "pure Gospel Ministry" and "supplying the poor with the Holy Scriptures." Two meetings were to be held each year, with a committee of twenty-one to act for the Association between the stated meetings.

A divided church was mourned as detrimental to the cause of Christ. The evils of division were pointed out.

What awful and distressing effects have those sad divisions produced! what aversions, what reproaches, what backbitings, what evil surmisings, what angry contentions, what enmities, what excommunications, and even persecution! . . . Thus, while professing Christians bite and devour one another, they are consumed one of another, or fall a prey to the righteous judgments of God; meantime, the truly religious of all parties are grieved, the weak stumbled, the graceless and profane hardened, the mouths of infidels opened to blaspheme religion . . . the Gospel of the blessed Jesus, is reduced to contempt, while multitudes, deprived of a Gospel ministry . . . fall an easy prey to seducers, and so become the dupes of almost unheard-of delusions.[6]

The core of the "Address" is a series of thirteen propositions. (It is suggested that these propositions be read and discussed in class.) These center in three basic concepts: (1) division and schism in the body of Christ is sin, being anti-Christian, anti-Scriptural, and anti-natural; (2) the Bible is all-sufficient as God's ultimate revelation and is the only adequate standard for doctrine, polity, and life; a truly Christian spirit is manifested through mutual love and forbearance.

The "Appendix" is explanatory and defensive. It seeks to clarify further the Association's attitude toward and relation to the religious world, and, as far as possible, to prevent misunderstandings of its purpose. Objections are anticipated and answered. It is clearly shown that the position taken by the Association is not latitudinarian; in fact, to accept the Word of God as the only standard for faith and practice is the only guard against being too broad—or too narrow. The folly of making opinions tests of fellowship or the ground for discipline is pointed out.

Two projects designed to aid the work of the Association are suggested in the "Postscript": the preparation of a "Christian Catechism" and the launching of a religious periodical. The catechism would be "an exhibition of that complete system of faith and duty expressly contained in the sacred oracles; respecting the doctrine, worship, discipline, and government of the christian church" (Centennial edition, p. 55). The periodical, to bear the name *Christian Monitor*, would be used "in detecting and exposing the various anti-Christian enormities, innovations and corruptions, which infect the christian church" (p. 55). The Christian Association did not live long enough to implement these proposals, but they were later objectified by Alexander Campbell in the *Christian System* and the *Christian Baptist*.

Questions

1. How did Thomas Campbell come to be a preacher in the Seceder Presbyterian Church?
2. How was he affected by the divisions among the Seceders and what did he do about them?
3. When and why did he emigrate to America?
4. Why did the Chartiers Presbytery oppose Thomas Campbell?
5. What action did the Presbyterian Synod take against him?
6. What was the purpose and program of the Christian Association of Washington?
7. What is the *Declaration and Address*? What now-famous slogan was set forth in it?
8. What basic principles of the Restoration movement are found in the *Declaration and Address*?

Notes

[1] R. Richardson, *Memoirs of Alexander Campbell*, Vol. I, p. 23.
[2] *Ibid.*, p. 229.
[3] *Ibid.*, p. 229.
[4] *Ibid.*, p. 232.
[5] *Ibid.*, p. 237.
[6] C. A. Young, *Historical Documents Advocating Christian Union*, pp. 80, 85.

CHAPTER 5

The Campbell Movement
Alexander Campbell

Alexander Campbell—farmer, teacher, preacher, statesman, postmaster, author, editor, debater—is undoubtedly the dominant figure in the history of the Restoration movement. So great was his influence and fame that those who disagreed with and opposed him gave the name "Campbellism" to the system of doctrine that he and others taught, and they dubbed his associates "Campbellites."

EARLY LIFE AND EDUCATION

Alexander Campbell, son of Thomas and Jane Corneigle Campbell, was born near Ballymena, County Antrim, Ireland, September 12, 1788. As already noted, his mother was a descendant of the French Huguenots who fled their home country when the Edict of Nantes, the "great charter of Huguenot rights" made by Henry IV in 1598, was revoked by Louis XIV in 1685.

Campbell's boyhood was spent on a farm near Rich Hill, some ten miles from the town of Newry, where his father located and lived while serving the Seceder Presbyterian Church at Ahorey. His education began in an elementary school at Market Hill and was continued in an academy taught by his uncles, Archibald and Enos Campbell. His father, a very successful teacher as well as a Seceder preacher, personally supervised a considerable portion of his son's education.

In this early period young Campbell manifested little of that devotion to study and learning that was to mark his later life and make him an outstanding leader in many areas. He was interested in games and in hunting and fishing. Because of his lack of interest in educational pursuits, his father set him to labor with those hired to do the farming, hoping that he might be benefited both physically and mentally.

This decision of the father proved to be a wise one. The physical labor helped Alexander to develop a good, strong body, which served him so well in the rigorous schedule that he later followed in America. And within a few years he lost much of his interest in former pastimes and turned his attention to study. He vowed to become "one of the best scholars in the kingdom." Under his father's guidance he read extensively in literature, philosophy, and religion. Having a ready memory, he stored many choice passages from the poets and other literature in his mind for instant recall when needed. He was introduced to the works of the philosopher John Locke, such as his *Essay on the Human Understanding,* and was greatly influenced by the Lockeian philosophical system. He also studied French, Latin, and Greek under his father's tutelage.

Thomas and Jane Campbell were both greatly concerned about their own and their children's spiritual life. The Bible occupied a prominent place in their home. Family worship was conducted daily. Each member of the family memorized a selection from the Bible each day, recited it during the period of worship in the evening, and discussed it afterward. These verses were given again in the family worship conducted during the evening of the Lord's Day.

Alexander was seventeen years of age when his father opened an academy in Rich Hill, only a short distance from where the family was living. The house into which they moved in Rich Hill served a double purpose, providing a home for the family and rooms for the classes. The son served as an assistant in the academy and also continued to study under the direction of his father.

About this time he became more concerned about religious matters, especially his own spiritual condition. The Seceders were Calvinistic in doctrine. Salvation, according to their teaching, involved the sinner's search for God and receiving His assurance that the promise of redemption applied to him personally. Campbell has left the following record of his "religious experience":

From the time that I could read the Scriptures, I became convinced that Jesus was the Son of God. I was also fully persuaded that I was a sinner, and must obtain pardon through the merits of Christ or be lost for ever. This caused me great distress of soul, and I had much exercise of mind under the awakenings of a guilty conscience. Finally, after many strugglings, I was enabled to put my trust in the Saviour, and to *feel* my reliance on him as the only Saviour of sinners. From the moment that I was able to feel this reliance on the Lord Jesus Christ, I obtained and enjoyed peace of mind.[1]

The new convert was received into the Seceder Church at Ahorey, the congregation to which his father ministered.

Thomas Campbell soon made known his desire for his son to become a minister. Alexander was not fully persuaded that this was the work to which his life should be given; nevertheless, he turned his attention to the reading of theology and church history.

A review of the historical record of the Roman Catholic Church, with her arrogant claims of supremacy and power, gross immorality, and persecution of other religious groups, repelled him. Personal observation only substantiated what he read. He was scarcely more favorably impressed by the cold, worldly activities of the Anglicans. Divisions in the church, which were accompanied by bickering, strife, and efforts for advancement of party, greatly perturbed him. He watched with sympathetic interest his father's efforts for reunion among the Seceders.

SHIPWRECK . . . AND DECISION

The excessive labors of Thomas Campbell as he worked at three jobs—preaching, teaching, farming—impaired his health. His physician recommended a sea voyage as an aid to the restoration of his health. He resolved to go to America and, when settled, have his family join him there. Alexander already had expressed a desire to go to this new country some day. Accordingly, in 1807 the father, leaving the academy and the family in the hands of his eldest son, set sail for America. When the session of the academy was finished, Alexander joined the teaching staff of his uncle Archibald in the school he was conducting at Newry.

In March, 1808, the long-awaited letter from the father was received, informing the family that all things were now ready and they should join him. An epidemic of smallpox, which affected the children of the family, delayed preparations for leaving. Finally, arrangements were completed, and on October 1, 1808, the family set sail on the *Hibernia* from Londonderry.

Their trip was again interrupted, however, when the *Hibernia* was blown off its course. The ship was brought into a bay of the island of Islay, where it lay anchored for almost three days. On the night of October 7 the winds became so strong that the anchors would not hold, and the ship was blown upon a rock and began to fill with water. For a time it seemed that all would be lost, but when the masts were cut down the ship righted itself and was able to ride out the storm.

This was a significant experience for Alexander Campbell. Having done all that he could for the safety and comfort of his family, he sat down upon the stump of one of the masts and gave serious thought to his life: past, present, and future. This was his hour of decision. He solemnly vowed that if God spared his life he would dedicate it completely to His service.

45

Help came with the dawning of the new day. The inhabitants of the island perceived the plight of the ship, and by heroic efforts succeeded in saving all the passengers. The islanders proved most hospitable, caring for the needs and comfort of these strangers to their isle. The family settled on the island, Alexander returned to the ship to salvage as much of their personal belongings as possible, including the books that he valued greatly. Since the journey could not be continued immediately, the Campbell family decided to spend the time of waiting in the city of Glasgow. Here the son would have an opportunity to study at the university which his father had attended.

GLASGOW—GENERAL AND RELIGIOUS EDUCATION

Alexander took some letters of introduction with him to Glasgow. The letters were written by those on the island who had become acquainted with this young man and were impressed by his talents and personality. He presented one of these letters to Greville Ewing, head of the Haldanean theological institute in Glasgow and minister in an Independent Church. Ewing proved to be a most courteous and kindly gentleman and a warm and considerate friend.

The few months spent in Glasgow were to prove very significant for Alexander Campbell. He enrolled in the university for study in Greek, French, logic, and philosophy. He read widely in poetry, ethics, natural history, philosophy, and theology, copying many passages from the books he read into notebooks for future use. In addition to pursuing his own program of study he found time to teach classes in Latin, grammar, and arithmetic, thus helping to take care of the expenses for his education.

Knowledge gained through study in those branches of learning related to the arts and sciences were important to the eager student. But they were secondary in importance to the impact made on his life through association and discussion with leaders, especially Greville Ewing, in the Scottish movement for a return to primitive Christianity as revealed in the New Testament. Since Campbell was later accused of being a Haldanean and a Sandemanian, perhaps a brief outline of the rise and development of their reformatory movements will be helpful.

John Glas was a minister in the Church of Scotland. About 1730, while serving as the minister at Tealing, his connection with the established church was severed and he formed an Independent Church. Within four years congregations had been established in Dundee, Perth, and Edinburgh. Robert Sandeman, the son-in-law of Glas, was associated with him. The churches established by these men were congregational in government. The Old and New Testaments were accepted as the complete revelation of the will of God for man and the perfect rule of conduct for Christians. They taught that "bishop" and "elder" referred to the same office or person. Elders were the overseers of the congregation and deacons ministered in material things. Apostolic succession, as well as all spiritual or religious distinctions between "clergy" and "laity," were denied. Sprinkling was accepted as the "mode" of baptism and was administered to believers and their children. They emphasized the memorial character of the Lord's Supper, communed weekly, and practiced closed Communion. The holy kiss and feet washing were made part of the congregational life. Members were subject to a ready and exacting discipline. For some reason, the Glasites, or Sandemanians, never became a popular or numerous group.

Archibald McLean and Robert Carmichael were founders of the Scotch Baptists. McLean left the Church of Scotland to join the Glasites in 1761, and Carmichael forsook the Anti-Burgher Seceders for the same fellowship in 1762. They remained with this group only a year, withdrawing because of dissatisfaction over the handling of certain disciplinary problems. The churches they established after their withdrawal followed the doctrinal pattern of the Glasites in most points. However, they did repudiate infant baptism and practiced immersion instead of sprinkling. From Scotland the Scotch Baptists spread into England and Wales. This body was later greatly disturbed and divided over the necessity for pastors in the constitution of a church and the right to celebrate the Lord's Supper when no elders were present.

The Haldane brothers, Robert and James, began a movement for reform in the Church of Scotland resembling that of John Wesley in the Church of England in its original purpose, but eventually paralleling the Glasites in doctrinal emphases. They were wealthy businessmen and used their money freely in attempts to revitalize the spiritual life and to promote evangelistic and missionary fervor in the established church. Efforts to promote missionary programs for India and Africa were unsuccessful. They organized the "Society for Propagating the Gospel at Home" and brought to Scotland Rowland Hill, the great English evangelist, to stir their countrymen with his earnest evangelism. Lay preaching was encouraged and theological schools established for the training of these preachers. The Haldanes left the Church of Scotland in 1799 and organized an Independent Church in Edinburgh, James becoming the pastor. They made many converts, and churches multiplied rapidly. Ten years had not passed, however, before the Haldanean forces were split over baptism. Out of the controversy over baptism eventually came the Congregational Church and the Baptist Church Union. The Haldanes themselves were immersed.

AN UNUSED COMMUNION TOKEN

The study of the philosophical systems of John Locke and Thomas Reid, of the Scottish "Common Sense" school of philosophy, undoubtedly had its effect on Campbell. His concept of faith as the belief of testimony and the reasonable nature of the Christian system and the Bible, as opposed to the irrational concept of faith he encountered in the Calvinistic system and the mystical and allegorical interpretations of the Word, were furthered by these eminent philosophers.

Alexander had opportunities to become acquainted with the teaching of the Independents through representatives who visited Rich Hill, including such men as Rowland Hill, James Haldane, Alexander Carson, and John Walker. He later indicated that his own doctrinal positions were much like those of John Walker.

While at Glasgow, Campbell was again exposed to Haldanean teaching through Greville Ewing, who was an associate of the Haldanes. While Ewing agreed with them in most doctrinal points, including their emphasis on restoring the church as it is set forth in the New Testament, he differed from their immersionist views, holding that sprinkling was equally acceptable as the fulfillment of this ordinance. Campbell often joined others in the Ewing home for informal discussions of various religious issues. He also attended Ewing's Sunday evening services quite frequently, listening to sermons which for clarity and warmth contrasted greatly with the cold and stilted messages he heard from the Seceder preacher on Sunday mornings.

Campbell became more and more sympathetic with the independents' position and more and more dissatisfied with Seceder Presbyterianism. But it seemed that he could not bring himself to sever his connection with this body. How much the fact that his father was a sincere Seceder minister affected his thinking we do not know, but in all probability this was one of the factors which he gave consideration, since he respected and honored him so greatly.

Although he was greatly concerned over his changing religious concepts and though he disapproved of many doctrines and practices of the Seceders, he successfully passed the examination that preceded the semiannual Communion service and was given a metallic token that entitled him to commune.

The hour for Communion came. A perplexed and uncertain Alexander Campbell was present with his Communion token. Could he conscientiously commune with others in a religious system that he no longer accepted? He waited until the last table in order to postpone his decision as long as possible. When he could delay no longer, he cast his token into the plate and left without communing!

This act, which to the casual observer might have seemed trivial and unimportant, marked Alexander Campbell's break from Presbyterianism and his determination to follow a new course. Perhaps in the uncertain light of this early dawn of the all-importance and all-sufficiency of Biblical truth Campbell could see only the dim outlines of the new road he had chosen to follow, but the light of God's Word was to grow brighter and brighter until it clearly illuminated even the far reaches of the highway of religious reformation, which he was to travel until death ended his journey.

REUNION OF THE CAMPBELL FAMILY IN AMERICA

Following the close of the session at the university, Campbell spent five weeks at Helensburgh tutoring children of some of his newfound friends in Glasgow. He returned to the city to complete arrangements for the trip to America. The family left Scotland aboard the *Latonia* on August 3, 1809. Although the ship sprang a leak and had to ride out several rather severe storms during the voyage, they arrived safely in New York on September 29, 1809.

The Campbells took the stage from New York to Philadelphia, arriving on October 7. After spending Sunday and a major portion of Monday in Philadelphia, they departed by wagon for Washington, some 350 miles away. Meanwhile, Thomas Campbell had set out to meet his loved ones. On October 19, 1809, somewhere on the road in western Pennsylvania, the family was reunited. Their journey ended at their new home some three days later.

At the time of the reunion neither father nor son knew that the other had renounced Presbyterianism. There may have been some reticence on the part of the son to make known his changed religious views. The father soon recounted his experiences in America, including his trials before presbytery and synod, his repudiation of both, and his continuing work as an independent minister. In turn, the son shared his religious experiences and his decision at Glasgow. They rejoiced greatly because of their unity of religious convictions. Alexander was delighted with the principles and program incorporated in the *Declaration and Address*. While Thomas Campbell had outlined the principles of restoration, his son was to propagate and defend them.

INFANT BAPTISM—A PERPLEXING PROBLEM

When the principle, "Where the Scriptures speak, we speak; where the Scriptures are silent, we are silent," was first announced in the home of Abraham Altars, as already noted it was quickly pointed out that this would put an end to the practice of infant baptism. At that time, Thomas Campbell said, "Of course, if infant baptism be not found in the Scripture, we can have nothing to do with it." But apparently he made no attempt to justify infant baptism on Scriptural grounds, relegating it to the realm of the "non-essentials" as a matter of private opinion. He said that he saw no reason to baptize those again who had been sprinkled in infancy; this was to take them out of the church in order to bring them in again.

James Foster, a member of the Christian Association, had become convinced that infant baptism was without Scriptural warrant before leaving Ireland for America. He believed that Campbell's rule should be applied to infant baptism. Richardson records the following conclusion to a discussion of infant baptism between Foster and Campbell:

"Father Campbell, how could you, in the absence of any authority in the Word of God, baptize a child in the name of the Father, and of the Son, and of the Holy Spirit?" . . . [Campbell's] face colored, he became for a moment irritated, and said in reply, in an offended tone: "Sir, you are the most intractable person I ever met."

Thomas Campbell strongly opposed divisions in the body of Christ. If at all possible, he wanted to avoid accusations of opposing divisions while fostering a new one through the Christian Association. Therefore, with the consent of the Association and a disregard for his son's pessimistic attitude concerning the venture, he presented the plan and program of the Christian Association to the Presbyterian Synod of Pittsburg and petitioned that body "to be taken into Christian and ministerial communion." The synod considered the petition, refusing admittance on the grounds that the course proposed by the Association would promote division instead of union, degrade the ministerial character, permit errors in doctrine, and corrupt discipline. "And further," they added, "for the above

50

and many other important reasons, it was resolved, that Mr. Campbell's request to be received into ministerial and Christian communion cannot be granted."[3]

When Campbell asked for a clarification of the "important reasons" indicated in this statement, among other things the synod indicated his irregular position concerning infant baptism: "For declaring that the administration of baptism to infants is not authorized by scriptural precept or example, and is a matter of indifference, yet administering that ordinance while holding such an opinion."[4]

Alexander Campbell preached his first sermon July 15, 1810, and soon became a popular preacher. He preached strictly as an independent. Though nominally a Presbyterian, he had affiliated with no religious body after coming to America. He preached without ordination or license, dedicated to the propagation of "simple, evangelical Christianity."

This young preacher was to become the leader in the application of the rule announced by his father. He had expressed full agreement with the principles set forth in the *Declaration and Address*. Yet, at this time, he was not quite ready to have this rule strictly applied to infant baptism. In a sermon on November 1, 1810, he argued that infant baptism was nowhere expressly enjoined, and that it should be made a matter of forbearance, even as circumcision was in the apostolic church. Again in June of the following year he said: "As I am sure it is unscriptural to make this matter a term of communion, I let it *slip*. I wish to think and let think on these matters."[5]

Alexander Campbell discussed baptism with a Baptist preacher in the home of his future father-in-law, but was unsatisfied with his showing. He examined the case for infant baptism as presented in the published works of its advocates and then turned to the Greek New Testament. But, although convinced that infant baptism and sprinkling had no Scriptural foundation or support, he was unwilling to make a practical application of his conclusions.

IMMERSION OF THE CAMPBELLS

The baptismal issue was climaxed when Alexander Campbell's first child was born and the matter of her baptism was considered. Further study of the subject, action, and purpose of baptism led him to repudiate infant sprinkling and accept believer's baptism. He was *now* ready to act on his conviction.

Matthias Luce, a Baptist preacher, finally agreed to baptize

Alexander Campbell and his wife upon the profession of their faith in Christ and without the relation of a "religious experience" according to Baptist custom. Thomas Campbell and his wife and their daughter, Dorothea, also decided to be immersed. Both father and son addressed the assembled crowd before the baptisms. Two others, Mr. and Mrs. James Hanen, requested baptism. These seven then were baptized by Mr. Luce in Buffalo Creek.

Questions

1. Describe the early life and education of Alexander Campbell.
2. When and how did he decide to become a minister?
3. What was the significance of the year he spent at Glasgow—educationally? religiously?
4. What significance may we attach to his refusal to use the Communion token just before coming to America?
5. Why were Thomas and Alexander Campbell so reluctant to give up the practice of infant baptism?
6. What event led Alexander Campbell to study infant baptism in the light of the New Testament?
7. Who baptized Alexander Campbell?
8. Name the others who were baptized at the same time. Describe the occasion and the baptisms.

Notes

[1]Richardson, *Memoirs of Alexander Campbell,* Vol. I, p. 49.
[2]*Ibid.,* p. 240.
[3]*Ibid.,* p. 327.
[4]*Ibid.,* p. 328.
[5]*Ibid.,* p. 392.

CHAPTER 6

Association With
the Baptists

Thomas Campbell found fellowship and opportunity for spiritual service in the Christian Association after his separation from the Seceder Presbyterians. Those of the Association who were church members continued to hold membership in different congregations, while joining together for the promotion of "simple evangelical Christianity." Rebuffed by the Presbyterian Synod of Pittsburgh, representing the main body of Presbyterians, and having little hope of finding acceptance elsewhere, Campbell and the Association were forced to consider their future course.

BRUSH RUN CHURCH

Brush Run Church Constituted

Alexander Campbell, in his reply to the statement of the Synod of Pittsburgh at the semiannual meeting of the Christian Association in November following the rejection of the petition for admission into the synod, intimated that if all doors were closed the Association might be compelled to organize and function as a church. No other course seemed to be open to them, so on May 4, 1811, the Brush Run Church was constituted. At this meeting Thomas Campbell asked this question of those who desired to become members of the new congregation: "What is the meritorious cause of a sinner's acceptance with God?" Thirty of the prospective new members gave satisfactory answers to the question and were enrolled as members; two were rejected.

Thomas Campbell was chosen the first elder, four deacons were selected, and Alexander Campbell was licensed to preach at this organizational meeting. Eight months later, January, 1812, Alexander Campbell was ordained to the gospel ministry. His ordination certificate was signed, "Thomas Campbell, Senior minister of the First Church of the Christian Association of Washington, meeting at Crossroads and Brush Run, Washington county, Pennsylvania."[1]

Brush Run Church and Immersion

The Brush Run Church began as an independent and autonomous church body. In their congregational capacity they selected their own leaders. The Lord's Supper was observed weekly. The Bible was designated their only guide in doctrine and life.

At the first service following the organization it was noted that some who had answered Thomas Campbell's question satisfactorily and were considered members of the Brush Run Church did not participate in the Communion. When questioned, they indicated an unwillingness to commune when they had not been baptized. Not one of the three—Joseph Bryant, Margaret Fullerton, and Abraham Altars—had been sprinkled when a child, or received baptism in any form later in life. They desired to be immersed.

While Thomas and Alexander Campbell were willing "to think and let think" on the validity of infant baptism, and had not been immersed themselves, the right of these to be immersed was recognized. At the appointed hour a large group gathered at a fairly deep pool in Buffalo Creek for the baptisms. In one respect at least these baptisms were rather unusual, as may be seen from the following account:

The pool was narrow, and so deep that the water came up to the shoulders of the candidates when they entered it. Thomas Campbell, then, without going into the water, stood on a root that projected over the edge of the pool, and bent down their heads until they were buried in the liquid grave, repeating at the same time, in each case, the baptismal formula.[2]

Alexander Campbell's decision to be immersed was significant for himself, his family, the Brush Run Church, and the Restoration movement. His search for the truth in regard to infant baptism resulted in five conclusions: infant baptism is without Biblical command or example; a believer is the only proper subject for baptism; immersion is the only "mode" of baptism found in the Bible; Alexander Campbell had not been Scripturally baptized; and Alexander Campbell would be immersed.

The baptism of Alexander Campbell and his wife, his father and mother, his sister Dorothea, and Mr. and Mrs. James Hanen made seven more immersed believers in the Brush Run Church. The Sunday following their baptism thirteen more members of the church requested immersion. Within a short period of time still others expressed a desire to be immersed. No effort was made to force every member to be immersed, but those who did not want to do so withdrew.

The fact that the church at Brush Run became a congregation of immersed believers had two far-reaching results. First, it led to bitter antagonism on the part of pedobaptists in their area. The Presbyterians particularly took it almost as a personal affront and challenge. Mr. Richardson tells us that

Misrepresentations of all kinds were freely circulated amongst the people; friendships were broken off; the ties of family relationship were weakened, and the discord of religious controversy invaded the quietude of the most secluded habitations. . . . The opposition, however, by no means confined itself to private intercourse, or even to the pulpit, but manifested itself in business relations, in the withdrawal of custom from members whose callings were dependent upon public patronage, and in slights at public gatherings whenever it was supposed an indignity might be safely offered to any member present. . . . It happened, more than once, that while Thomas Campbell was baptizing individuals who came forward from time to time to unite with the church, sticks and stones were thrown into the water from amidst the crowd assembled; imprecations also would sometimes be heard, and even threats of personal violence.[3]

But if the repudiation of infant baptism and sprinkling and the practice of immersion filled pedobaptists with hatred and animosity, it found for them some new friends among the Baptists. The Campbells had been baptized by Matthias Luce, a Baptist preacher; they were now "baptists" and protagonists for the Baptist position in relation to the form of this ordinance. Alexander Campbell was invited to preach in their churches. Members of the Redstone Baptist Association began to urge the Campbells to bring the Brush Run Church into their Association.

AFFILIATION WITH THE REDSTONE BAPTIST ASSOCIATION

The friendly overtures from members of the Redstone Association met with little interest or favor at first. While Alexander Campbell had been welcomed by the Baptist "laity," and was favorably impressed by their consecration and piety, he had little respect for most of the "clergy," whom he characterized as "narrow, contracted, illiberal and uneducated . . . little men in a big office."[4] But he soon learned that the Baptists themselves were greatly dissatisfied with their leaders.

The question of affiliation with Redstone was finally laid before the Brush Run Church for their consideration and decision. The congregation applied for admission to the Redstone Association, providing they would be received on their own terms. A need was felt for fellowship and for avoiding, if at all possible, the accusation of creating another religious body while pleading for the union of Christians. Alexander Campbell later reported:

Some eight or ten pages of large dimensions, exhibiting our remonstrance against all human creeds as bonds of union or communion among Christian churches, and expressing a willingness, on certain conditions, to co-operate or to unite with that Association; provided only, and always, that we should be allowed to preach and teach whatever we learned from the Holy Scriptures, regardless of any creed or formula in Christendom.[5]

While a few objected to receiving Brush Run on these conditions, an overwhelming majority favored their admission. So the Brush Run Church was welcomed into the Redstone Baptist Association in the fall of 1813.

"Likes" and "Unlikes"

There were a number of similarities in the faith and practice of the Brush Run Church and the Baptist churches composing the Redstone Association. Among these "likes" were the following: the Bible the final authority in religion; autonomy of the local congregation, observance of the Lord's Supper; repudiation of sprinkling; immersion of believers; ordination of the ministry; divinity of Christ; the atonement; resurrection of the dead; the ultimate happiness of the righteous and eternal punishment of the wicked.

There were also "unlikes" in relation to some of these points of agreement, as well as in other areas. They differed as to the utility and use of creeds, divisions of the Bible, the purpose of baptism, the administrator of baptism, frequency of the Lord's Supper, operation of the Holy Spirit in conversion, requirements for church membership. Many of these differences were made apparent through the preaching and writings of Alexander Campbell.

While professing allegiance to the Bible as final authority, the Baptists had adopted the *Philadelphia Confession of Faith*, a Calvinistic document, as the standard of Baptist orthodoxy and the basis for union and communion. Brush Run repudiated the authority and expediency of all such human documents, proclaiming the all-sufficiency of the Word of God.

The Baptists made little or no distinction between the Old and New Testaments, or between the Jewish and Christian dispensations. The *Declaration and Address* proclaimed the unique character of the New Testament for the Christian age. Alexander Campbell enraged his opponents and alienated others in the Baptist ranks with his clear distinction between the old and new covenants in his *Sermon on the Law* in 1816.

The Baptists immersed *because* the candidate's sins *were already forgiven;* Brush Run immersed *unto* or *in order to* the remission of sins. The Baptists held that only an ordained minister should baptize; Brush Run taught that any Christian might, in keeping with the commission of Christ, baptize a penitent believer.

According to the Baptists, the Holy Spirit operated *directly* upon the sinner in conversion, bestowing saving faith to those elected by God and predestined to eternal life. Brush Run taught that the Holy Spirit operated only through the Word in converting sinners, that faith came through believing the testimony found in the Bible.

The Baptists required the relation of a religious "experience," indicating the fact of their regeneration, before baptism and admission into the church by vote of the congregation. Brush Run simply called upon sinners to believe in Christ and, having confessed this faith, to be baptized. All those who believed and were baptized were extended "the right hand of fellowship."

Sermon on the Law (1816)

Alexander Campbell continued to preach among the Baptists. His reformatory doctrines were accepted by many but met with increased antagonism on the part of others.

A meeting of the Redstone Association was held at Cross Creek, Virginia, the last of August, 1816. A petition was introduced for the admission into the Association of a small congregation of immersed believers gathered together by Thomas Campbell in Pittsburgh, where he was teaching. The petition was rejected because it was "not presented according to the constitution of this Association." However, Thomas Campbell was given a seat in the meeting, and an article on "The Trinity," which he had prepared by request of the Association, was accepted and ordered to be printed in the minutes.

Many of the people and some preachers, desiring to hear Alexander Campbell, nominated him as one of the speakers; but Elder John Pritchard, claiming the right as the host preacher to name the speakers, substituted the name of Elijah Stone of Ohio for that of Campbell. When Stone became ill Campbell was asked to preach, and delivered his now famous *Sermon on the Law*.

This sermon was based on Romans 8:3. In it he pointed out the meaning of "the law," limitations of "the law," reasons for these limitations, and how God remedied the defects of "the law" through Christ. He argued that the complete Law of Moses was nullified, superseded by the gospel of Christ. The old dispensation passed away, making room for a new dispensation having a new covenant, new sacrifices, new priests, and new forms of worship.

Campbell later told readers of the *Harbinger*, "This unfortunate sermon afterwards involved me in a seven years' war with some members of the said Association, and became a matter of much debate."[6] An immediate move to have the doctrine set forth in the sermon condemned by the Association failed. It was printed, however, and at the next meeting of the Redstone Association it was brought forth as sufficient cause to try its author on charges of heresy. While the charges were dropped at that time, they were repeated before the Association for several years.

Campbell considered his appearance before the Redstone Association in 1816 to deliver this sermon providential. He later wrote: "He [Stone, the speaker first selected] providentially was suddenly seized by sickness."[7] The sermon also had great importance for the future of the Restoration movement according to Campbell: "It is, therefore, highly probable to my mind, that but for the persecution begun on the alleged heresy of this sermon, whether the present reformation had ever been advocated by me."[8]

ALEXANDER CAMPBELL'S DEBATES

Alexander Campbell engaged in five public debates on religious subjects. At first he was reluctant to enter into a public discussion of religion; he agreed with his father, who felt that Christianity required a demonstration rather than a debate. While limitations of space do not permit a discussion of the lines of argument in these debates, a list of opponents, their religious affiliations, places and dates of the debates, and subjects discussed is included here.

John Walker, Presbyterian. Mount Pleasant, Ohio; June 19, 20, 1820. Mode and subjects of baptism.

William L. MacCalla, Presbyterian. Washington, Kentucky; October 15-21, 1823. Mode and subjects of baptism.

Robert Owen, skeptic. Cincinnati, Ohio; April 13-21, 1829. Evidences of Christianity.

John B. Purcell, Roman Catholic. Cincinnati, Ohio; January 13-21, 1837. Roman Catholicism.

Nathan L. Rice, Presbyterian. Lexington, Kentucky; November 15–December 1, 1843. Mode, subjects, and purpose of baptism; operation of the Holy Spirit; creeds; Christian union.

In the first two debates Campbell appeared as the champion of the Baptist cause, in the one with Owen, as the defender of Christianity, in his debate with Purcell, as the representative of Protestantism, and with Rice, as a leader of the Restoration movement.

Most Significant Debate

All of these debates were important, but the first proved most significant for Campbell and the religious world for a number of reasons. It revealed his aptitude for and power in the public discussion of religious issues. It convinced Campbell that debating was a legitimate and excellent means for exposing error and disseminating truth. Doors were opened to him for preaching in Baptist churches. The challenge issued at the close of the debate led to the discussion with MacCalla, which served to enhance further the stature of Campbell among the Baptists and gave him entrance into many Baptist churches in Kentucky, where his reformatory views spread rapidly. Here, also, he first became acquainted with B. W. Stone. The publication of the debate spread Campbell's views on baptism much more widely than they otherwise might have been at this time.

Results

Some ten years later Campbell revealed two results of this debate, which were most significant for the Restoration movement. In the concluding article of the *Christian Baptist* he wrote:

An unsuccessful effort by my father to reform the presbytery and synod to which he belonged, made me despair of reformation. I gave it up as a hopeless effort: but did not give up speaking in public assemblies upon the great articles of christian faith and practice. In the hope, the humble hope, of erecting a single congregation with which I could enjoy the social institutions, I labored. I had not the remotest idea of being able to do more than this.

.   .   .   .

It was not until after I discovered the effects of that discussion that I began to hope that something might be done to rouse this generation from its supineness and spiritual lethargy. About two years afterwards I conceived the plan of this work, and thought I should make the experiment.[9]

WALTER SCOTT AND THE MAHONING ASSOCIATION

Walter Scott, successful teacher, evangelist, and editor, holds an important place in the early history of the Restoration movement. He was born in Moffat, Scotland, in 1796. His parents were members of the Church of Scotland. He received his higher education in the University of Edinburgh. At the request of an uncle, George Innes, he came to New York in 1818, finding employment as a Latin tutor in an academy. He soon left this position to travel west, arriving in Pittsburgh in 1819, where he became assistant to George Forrester in the academy that he conducted.

Forrester, also a Scotsman, had received religious training under the Haldanes before coming to America. In addition to conducting the academy he worked with a small congregation that he had established. Scott proved an apt pupil of Forrester in religious matters, soon forsook Presbyterianism, and was baptized by his teacher.

Scott devoted himself to his teaching and a study of the Bible. A tract issued by a Scottish Baptist Church in New York fell into his hands and he made a visit to this congregation. He was disappointed with their Calvinistic concepts. He was also disappointed with independent congregations that he visited in Baltimore and Washington. He returned to Pittsburgh and resumed teaching. The sudden death of Forrester by drowning gave Scott the oversight of the congregation in Pittsburgh. His study of the Bible led him to conclude that the messiahship of Jesus is the central fact of the Bible and the divine creed for Christians.

Scott and Alexander Campbell met in Pittsburgh in 1822; they became warm friends. It was at Scott's suggestion that Campbell named his paper *The Christian Baptist* instead of *The Christian.* His contributions to this paper appeared over the name "Philip." In 1826 he moved to Steubenville, Ohio, to open an academy. He attended the meeting of the Mahoning Baptist Association the same year.

Evangelism was almost dead among the churches of the Mahoning Association. In 1827 fourteen churches reported thirty-four baptisms. Two churches, Wellsburg and Hiram, were responsible for more than half of these. Alexander Campbell suggested that Scott be called to evangelize for the Association, and he accepted. At his best the new evangelist was a superlative preacher, but on occasion he failed miserably.

Scott immediately began a careful and thorough study of the New Testament. He discovered the following "order" in conversion: faith, repentance, baptism, remission of sins, gift of the Holy Spirit (later to be known as Scott's "five-finger exercise"). He met with little success at first, but he persisted and was able to report some thousand additions at the annual meeting of the Association.

Under Scott's influence a great evangelistic movement based upon the messiahship of Christ and a clear presentation of the "plan" of salvation revealed in the New Testament swept the Western Reserve. There was no "mourner's bench," no call for a "religious experience." Individuals who confessed their faith that "Jesus is the Christ, the Son of God" were baptized "for the remission of sins." Baptist churches were being revitalized, and many Christian Churches (Newlight) were accepting Scott's program. Reports from the Western Reserve reached the Campbells, and Thomas went to see what was happening. He wrote his son:

We have long known the former (the theory), and have spoken and published many things *correctly concerning* the ancient gospel, its simplicity and perfect adaptation to the present state of mankind . . . but I must confess that, in respect to the *direct exhibition* and *application* of it for that blessed purpose, I am at present for the first time upon the ground where the thing has appeared to be *practically exhibited* to the proper purpose.[10]

At the meeting in Austintown in 1830, upon motion of John Henry, the Association voted itself out of existence and became merely an annual meeting.

SEPARATION FROM THE BAPTISTS

The union of the Brush Run Church with the Redstone Association was a shaky union at best. Refusal to abide by the *Philadelphia Confession* made permanent union doubtful. The *Sermon on the Law* alarmed many Baptists. Campbell's reform program, harsh criticisms of the clergy, and opposition to various practices of the Baptists were constant aggravations. His growing popularity and success angered many of the clergy. To many Baptists, Campbell was a dangerous man, guilty of heresy, and should be excluded from their fellowship. Special efforts were made to discredit him in the Redstone Association in 1823. He frustrated the attempt by obtaining letters for himself and about thirty members of the Brush Run Church and organizing a new congregation in Wellsburg. Since the new congregation did not belong to the Redstone Association, he was beyond its jurisdiction and power.

But the opposition would not be satisfied as long as Alexander Campbell and those tainted with "Campbellism" remained within the Baptist fold. In 1825 ten churches of the Redstone Association adhering to the *Philadelphia Confession* excluded thirteen churches, including Brush Run, from their fellowship. Baptist Associations in Kentucky, Pennsylvania, and Virginia soon purged their ranks of "Campbellites." By 1830, although the work of separation was not yet fully complete, the exclusion of the "Reforming Baptists" was rather well accomplished and the lines clearly drawn.

Alexander Campbell had said: "I do intend to continue my connection with this people so long as they will permit me to say what I believe; to teach what I am assured of, and to censure what is amiss in their views and practices." "This people" had determined that Alexander Campbell's program was intolerable.

Questions

1. Discuss the organization of the Brush Run Church. What question was asked each prospective member?
2. Describe Thomas Campbell's first immersions as minister of the Brush Run Church.
3. How did the Brush Run Church become a body of immersed believers? How did this affect the religious community?
4. On what basis did the Brush Run Church affiliate with the Redstone Baptist Association?
5. How were Brush Run Church and the Baptist churches alike? How did they differ?
6. What was the "Sermon on the Law?" What was its significance?
7. With whom did Alexander Campbell have public debates? What issues were discussed?
8. What contribution did Walter Scott make to the Restoration movement?

Notes

[1]Richardson, *Memoirs of Alexander Campbell,* Vol. I, p. 391.
[2]*Ibid.,* pp. 372, 373.
[3]*Ibid.,* p. 431.
[4]*Millennial Harbinger,* 1848, p. 345.
[5]*Ibid.,* p. 346.
[6]*Ibid.,* 1846, p. 493.
[7]*Ibid.,* 1846, p. 494.
[8]*Ibid.,* 1846, p. 493.
[9]*Christian Baptist,* Burnet edition., p. 664.
[10]William Baxter, *Life of Elder Walter Scott,* pp. 158, 159.

CHAPTER 7

Union of the Reformers and the Christians

The Stone movement in Kentucky antedated that led by the Campbells. It had been under way for a number of years before Thomas Campbell arrived in America. The *Last Will and Testament of the Springfield Presbytery* preceded the *Declaration and Address* by five years. While there were some differences between the Reformers under the leadership of the Campbells and the Christians who were associated with Stone, there were enough similarities to give hopes for a successful union of the two groups.

Barton Stone was a determined foe of partyism and an ardent advocate of Christian union. In a letter to the *Christian Palladium* in 1840 he stated his great concern for union in these words: "Christian union is my polar star. Here I stand as unmoved as the Allegheny mountains, nor can any thing drive me hence."[1]

Stone found some of the Presbyterians in North Carolina crossing party lines to associate with those of other denominations. The Orange Presbytery, which licensed Stone to preach, was rather liberal in the interpretation of certain Presbyterian doctrines, being influenced by such men as David Caldwell, William Hodge, and Henry Pattillo. And while teaching in Succoth Academy, at Washington, Georgia, Stone was closely associated with Hope Hull, who had been a sympathizer with James O'Kelly but had remained with the Methodists when the break finally came. Undoubtedly, he heard from Hull much about O'Kelly's fight for religious freedom and his plea for a return to the Bible. It is not particularly strange, then, to find Stone co-operating with Methodists and Baptists in the Kentucky revival, ignoring doctrinal issues and party lines in the evangelistic fervor of the hour.

Stone and others were unwilling to sacrifice their freedom in Christ and loyalty to His Word for Presbyterian exclusiveness and party standard. Withdrawal from the jurisdiction of the Synod of Kentucky and organization of the Springfield Presbytery were significant events. The new presbytery was much more liberal in its sentiments than those which had been forsaken. The growing conviction that division and partyism were destructive of vital Christianity soon led to the dissolution of the new presbytery. The *will* of this body, expressed through the *Last Will and Testament,* was "that this body die, be dissolved and sink into union with the body of Christ at large."

Alexander Campbell was also exposed to formative influences of Biblical emphasis and the unity of Christians. These were dominant notes in the preaching and work of his father, both in Ireland and America. The Haldanean concepts of Biblical Christianity, which he first heard at Rich Hill, were renewed through association with Greville Ewing and others while at Glasgow. In the *Declaration and Address,* with its Biblical and unitive emphases, Alexander Campbell found religious sentiments and aspirations that paralleled his own.

SIMILARITIES OF THE REFORMERS AND THE CHRISTIANS

Generally speaking, we find the views of Barton Stone reflected by the Christians and the views of Alexander Campbell representative of the Reformers.

All-sufficiency of the Scriptures and the Rejection of Creeds

Both Reformers and Christians insisted that the Bible must be the final authority, the deciding voice in all religious matters. Human creeds as tests of fellowship were vigorously opposed.

These positions are clearly stated in the *Last Will and Testament*: "We *will,* that the people henceforth take the Bible as the only sure guide to heaven; and as many as are offended with other books, which stand in competition with it, may cast them into the fire if they choose; for it is better to enter into life having one book, than having many to be cast into hell." Factions and party spirit within the body of Christ were believed to be "principally owing to the adoption of human creeds and forms of government."[2] Stone suggested that all creeds should be given to the "moles and bats."

In the *Declaration and Address* we find these expressions: "The Divine word is our standard"; "Nothing ought to be inculcated upon Christians as articles of faith; nor required of them as terms of communion, but what is expressly taught and enjoined upon them in the word of God"; the New Testament is a perfect "constitution

64

for the worship, discipline, and government of the New Testament Church."[3]

Emphasis on Unity

Thomas Campbell characterized divisions in the church as anti-Scriptural, anti-natural, and anti-Christian. Lest they be accused of starting a new party, he sought fellowship for himself and the Christian Association with the Synod of Pittsburgh. It was only after rejection of this petition, and there seemed no other alternative, that the Brush Run Church was organized. And when the opportunity came, the new congregation joined forces with the Baptists in the Redstone Association.

Nature of Faith

Stone and the Campbells had rejected the Calvinistic doctrine that faith is a miraculous gift of the Holy Spirit. Stone taught that there can be no faith without testimony. The "word of God is the foundation of faith," offering "sufficient evidence in itself to produce faith," which is *simply believing the testimony of God.*"[4] Alexander Campbell, whom many believe indebted to Locke for his concept of faith, defined faith as "the belief of testimony," or "the certainty of the experience of other persons."[5]

Baptism

Baptism was not an issue when Stone and others renounced the jurisdiction of the Synod of Kentucky. Before this break Robert Marshall became convinced that immersion of believers was Scriptural baptism. Attempting to correct his concept of baptism, Stone became convinced that Marshall was right. The excitement attending the Kentucky revival and the separation from the Presbyterians pushed consideration of baptism into the background for a time. Later, the matter came before the Kentucky Christians again. It was agreed that all who desired to do so should be immersed. Stone immersed David Purviance, Purviance baptized Reuben Dooley, and these baptized others. Stone was not immersed until later, although he and the other preachers continued to immerse their converts. While immersion was not made a test of fellowship among the Christians in Kentucky, it became the common practice.

Stone, through continued Biblical study, concluded that baptism was associated with the remission of sins and should be "administered in the name of Jesus to all believing penitents." While he preached this doctrine on occasion, he did not grasp its full significance.

65

He later wrote: "Into the spirit of the doctrine I was never fully led, until it was revived by Brother Alexander Campbell, some years after."[6]

Alexander Campbell struggled with the doctrine of baptism, but once fully convinced that infant baptism was unscriptural and that immersion was Scriptural baptism, he immediately sought out a Baptist preacher to immerse him. (Some point to the immersion of the Campbells as the time when the mantle of leadership in the Campbellian reformation passed from the father to the son.) The meaning and design of baptism in the Christian dispensation became increasingly clear to him, and through sermon, private discussion, public debate, and periodical contributions Campbell constantly challenged the religious world to give it the place and importance in the conversion of sinners that it was given in apostolic preaching and practice. The Reformers made immersion a requisite for church membership.

Autonomy of the Local Church

The Springfield Presbytery "willed" that the church resume her right of internal government, and the Christians continued to emphasize the freedom of the local congregations from all other sources of ecclesiastical authority. The Reformers were also jealous of the freedom of the local church. When Brush Run entered the Redstone Association, it was with the understanding that this Association had no authority to determine its doctrines and practices. The death of the Mahoning Association through the influence of Walter Scott was due to the repudiation of all extra-congregational bodies.

DIFFERENCES OF THE REFORMERS AND CHRISTIANS

Trinity

While both Reformers and Christians pointed out that the word "trinity" does not appear in the Bible, the former group were predominantly Trinitarian in theology while some of the latter seemed to be Unitarian.

Alexander Campbell conceived of God as having one divine nature and three manifestations. He writes of God's "plurality, relation, and society in himself" and of the "holy and incomprehensible relations in the Divinity."[7] In a critique of the Unitarians' doctrine of God published in the *Millennial Harbinger* for 1846, he wrote:

But who, of good sense, argues that these three persons are one person—one being! That God is one and plural, is just as evident as that he can be every where and no where . . . But we have a manifestation of God out of humanity in the Father, of God in humanity in the Son, and of God with humanity in the Holy Spirit.[8]

Stone was greatly confused by the doctrine of the Trinity as outlined in the *Westminster Confession.* He believed the orthodox Trinitarian theology to be unreasonable, without Scriptural revelation or support, and involving a divine relationship for which no suitable earthly analogy can be found. Yet he unhesitatingly affirmed his belief in the living God and in the pre-existence and divinity of Christ.

Because of his "unorthodox" view of the Trinity, which was shared by many of the Christians, Stone was opposed not only by Campbell and other Reformers, but also by many of the Protestant denominational leaders. Fundamental differences in this area of theology were to become a major factor in defeating overtures for unity between the Reformers and the New England Christians, as well as many congregations in other sections of the country.

Atonement

Stone's rejection of a vicarious or substitutionary atonement, a doctrine which he felt would justify either the Calvinistic concept of a limited atonement or the Universalists' teaching of salvation for all, led to extended oral and written discussions with Presbyterians and Reformers, including Alexander and Thomas Campbell. For Stone, the atonement was an "at-one-ment"; through the life and death of Jesus, God and men are reconciled.

According to Alexander Campbell, atonement is the *cause* and reconciliation the *effect* of the death of Christ. Concerning the sacrifice of Jesus, the Lamb of God, he wrote:

Sacrifice, as respects God, is a *propitiation*; as respects *sinners,* it is a *reconciliation*; as respects *sin,* it is an *expiation*; as respects the *saved* it is a *redemption.* . . . As a *propitiation* or atonement it is offered to God: not, indeed, to move his benevolence or to excite his mercy, but to render him propitious *according to law and justice.*[9]

The Name

Rice Haggard was convinced that the name "Christian" given to the disciples at Antioch (Acts 11:26) was the "new name, which the mouth of the Lord shall name" (Isaiah 62:2). He influenced both the O'Kelly secessionists from the Methodist Church and those who renounced Presbyterianism with Stone in Kentucky to adopt and use this name to the exclusion of all others.

Alexander Campbell denied that the word translated "called"

in Acts 11:26 indicated "divine appointment." Any Scriptural name was acceptable to Campbell, but he preferred the name "Disciples" or "Disciples of Christ" as being more ancient, more descriptive, more Scriptural, and more unappropriated. In the amplification of the fourth point he wrote: "Unitarians, Arians, and sundry other newly risen sects abroad, are zealous for the name *Christian*; while we are the only people on earth fairly and indisputably in the use of the title *Disciples of Christ*."[10]

"Disciples," "Disciples of Christ," and "Christians" were used to designate the followers of the Lord, and to some extent these names were used in referring to the adherents of the Restoration movement. "Christian Church" and "Church of Christ" have been almost exclusively used to designate local congregations.

Evangelism

The Christians were intensely evangelistic. The fervor of the Kentucky revival continued to characterize their work. On the other hand, the Campbells had done little to foster evangelism. Walter Scott, as the evangelist for the Mahoning Association, inaugurated an effective evangelistic program. His sane, logical, Scriptural approach to the conversion of sinners was radically different from the early emotional "mourner's bench" type of evangelism of the Christians.

UNION EFFORTS

The Christians, under the influence of Stone and others, antedated the Campbell movement among the Baptists in Kentucky by almost twenty years. The Campbellian influence, augmented by debate, personal tours, and the *Christian Baptist,* spread rapidly in Kentucky from about 1823, the time of the Campbell-MacCalla debate, and his reform doctrines became the cause of dissension among the Baptists. By 1830 the Campbells and all those suspected of "Campbellism" were being excluded from the Baptist fellowship.

Efforts Begin in Kentucky

Serious efforts to effect a union between the Reformers and the Christians began in Kentucky about 1831. Already there had been some association and fellowship between certain preachers of the two groups in Ohio. Recognizing their similarities and willing to forbear in their differences, the two congregations representing the Reformers and the Christians in Millersburg, near Cane Ridge and Paris, Kentucky, began communing together and finally became a united body in April, 1831.

John T. Johnson, who had been greatly influenced by Alexander Campbell, attempted reforms in the Baptist Church at Great Crossings, of which he was a member. Failing to accomplish his desires, he withdrew and established a church on reform principles. Barton Stone was the preacher of the Christian Church in nearby Georgetown. Personal contacts led to mutual esteem and love. Campbell wrote of the situation at Great Crossings: "We rejoice to hear that the utmost harmony and christian love prevail, not only amongst the disciples composing this congregation, but between them and the disciples meeting under the *Christian* name in connexion with brother Stone in Georgetown, nothwithstanding the sparrings between us editors."[11]

Union Discussed at Georgetown

In November, 1831, Raccoon John Smith, who was waging a battle for reform among the Baptists in Kentucky, was called to hold a meeting at Great Crossings. Johnson, Smith, Stone, and John Rogers (Christian) began discussing a union of the Reformers and Christians, and determined to make an effort to effect it. They announced meetings for the discussion of union at Georgetown on December 23-26, 1831, and for Lexington, December 30, 1831, through January 2, 1832.

At the meeting in Georgetown, Smith was selected to speak for the Reformers and Stone for the Christians. Smith had been opposing sectarianism and urging union in his preaching throughout this region. He expressed a willingness to forego all opinions or speculations in order to promote union and made clear his determination to use only Biblical terms for Biblical doctrines. He said:

While there is but one faith, there may be ten thousand opinions; and hence, if Christians are ever to be one, they must be one in faith, and not in opinion.

. . . .

While, for the sake of peace and Christian union, I have long since waived the public maintenance of any speculation I may hold, yet *not one Gospel fact, commandment, or promise, will I surrender for the world!*

Let us, then, my brethren, be no longer Campbellites or Stoneites, New Lights or Old Lights, or any other kind of *lights,* but let us all come to the Bible alone, as the only book in the world that can give us all the Light we need.[12]

Stone was deeply moved by the words of Smith. He expressed regret for his own speculations in the past and for their harmful effect upon himself and the church. He concluded: "I have not one objection to the ground laid down by him as the true scriptural basis of union among the people of God; and I am willing to give him, now and here, my hand."[13]

Union Achieved

While a hymn was being sung hand met hand in a pledge of brotherhood and fellowship. All joined together about the table of memory as one body on the Lord's Day. Williams writes of this union:

It was an equal and mutual pledge and resolution to meet on the Bible as on common ground, and to preach the Gospel rather than to propagate opinions. The brethren of Stone did not join Alexander Campbell as their leader, nor did the brethren of Campbell join Barton W. Stone as their leader; but each, having already taken Jesus the Christ as their only Leader, in love and liberty became one body; not Stoneites, or Campbellites; not Christians, or Disciples, distinctively as such; but Christians, Disciples, saints, brethren, and children of the same Father, who is God over all, and in all.[14]

In order to cement the union and to encourage it elsewhere, Stone took John T. Johnson (Reformer) as co-editor of the *Christian Messenger*. John Smith (Reformer) and John Rogers (Christian) were selected to ride together and visit the churches, in order to make them acquainted with what had happened and to persuade them to similar action.

Union in Indiana

About this time a union was being effected between the Christians and Reformers in eastern Indiana under the labors of John Longley (Christian) and John P. Thompson (Reformer). Longley wrote to Stone on December 24, 1831: "The Reforming Baptists and we are one here." An earlier movement for union had developed in southern Indiana under the leadership of John Wright, a Free-Will Baptist. Wright held that "all human creeds are heretical and schismatical," and that the Bible was a sufficient guide for all Christians. In 1819 he persuaded the Blue River Baptist Church to drop its creed and sustain itself on the Bible alone. Within two years the churches forming the Blue River Association had accepted Wright's position and disbanded as an association. The Dunkards and Newlights soon joined these reformers. By 1828 union was practically complete among these groups. Uniting with them later were the Regular Baptists forming the Silver Creek Association, influenced by Absalom and John T. Littell and Mordecai Cole.

Union in Tennessee and Illinois

The union movement reached into Tennessee. E. Sweat wrote from Lebanon: "On last Lord's day in July at a camp-meeting on Lock's Creek, Rutherford Co. Tenn. The Christian and reforming brethren united."[15]

In his report of a tour through the west in the fall of 1832, Stone indicated that union was under way also in Illinois:

We had very interesting meetings in Lawrenceville, Jacksonville, Carrolton, Rushville, Springfield, &c. of Illinois. In Jacksonville we witnessed a happy union of the two societies, Christians and Reformers, in one body or church. This church consists of 80 members.—There are many more who were not present.—In Jersey prairie about 50 of these two societies would unite on the same foundation the next Lord's day following. In Carrolton the same union was to take place at the same time.[16]

SOME CHRISTIANS REFUSE UNION

But the union was not to be consummated in some areas. The leadership of the eastern Christians, especially in the New England States and in some areas of Ohio, were opposed to any union with the "Campbellites." They objected to union on the grounds of Campbell's legalism and, particularly, his doctrine of baptism, which they chose to call "baptismal regeneration." Alexander Campbell was equally opposed to union with them. He classed them with the Unitarians and accused them of failing to give Christ His rightful place, of not recognizing His full deity.

Stone was under fire from both sides, but particularly from some of his "Christian" brethren who did not like Campbell. To their accusations that he favored "the errors of the Reformers," Stone replied:

I would prefer death to such a practice. The Reformers have, doubtless, errors, as fallible men—no doubt, we have also. . . . You may think I have seceded from the C. Church, because the Reformers and we, being on the same foundation, and agreeing to take the same name *Christian,* have united as one people. Is not this the very principle we have been pleading from the beginning? Is uniting with any people in this manner seceding from the church? In thus uniting do we agree to unite with all the opinions and errors of each other? . . . Have we by such union agreed to receive all their errors? No. In the great leading principles, or facts of the New Testament we agree, and cheerfully let each other have his opinions, as private property.[17]

Some years later, looking back on these early efforts for union, Stone indicated one reason for the failure to bring about a union of all the Christians and the Reformers. "This union, I have no doubt, would have been as easily effected in other States as in Kentucky," he wrote, "had there not been a few ignorant, head-

71

strong bigots on both sides, who were more influenced to retain and augment their party, than to save the world by uniting according to the prayer of Jesus."[18]

Questions

1. Who were the Reformers? Who were the Christians?
2. How were the Reformers and the Christians alike?
3. How did the Reformers and the Christians differ?
4. Describe the union meetings at Georgetown and Lexington, Kentucky. Who were the leaders?
5. In what two ways were these efforts at union promoted?
6. What difficulties would be encountered in a union of two such religious bodies as these?
7. Why did the union efforts succeed so well in Kentucky?
8. Why did the efforts at union not succeed with the Christians in the east?

Notes

[1]*Christian Palladium,* p. 286.
[2]Young, *Historical Documents Advocating Christian Union,* pp. 21, 22, 24.
[3]*Ibid.,* pp. 117, 108, 109.
[4]Rogers, *Biography of Eld. Barton W. Stone.* pp. 205, 206.
[5]*Millennial Harbinger,* 1837.
[6]Rogers, *Biography of Eld. Barton W. Stone,* p. 61.
[7]*The Christian System,* pp. 8, 12.
[8]*Millennial Harbinger,* 1846, p. 394.
[9]*The Christian System,* p. 23.
[10]*Millennial Harbinger,* 1839, p. 403.
[11]*Ibid.,* 1832, p. 29.
[12]J. A. Williams, *Life of Elder John Smith,* pp. 453, 454.
[13]*Ibid.,* p. 455.
[14]*Ibid.,* p. 456.
[15]*Christian Messenger,* 1832, p. 345.
[16]*Ibid.,* p. 347.
[17]*Ibid.,* 1833, p. 6.
[18]Rogers, *Biography of Eld. Barton W. Stone,* p. 78.

CHAPTER 8

Organizational Developments

EARLY ATTITUDES

In breaking away from the established ecclesiastical order of their day, the early leaders in the Restoration movement renounced the jurisdiction and questioned the legitimacy of authoritative religious organizations outside the local congregation.

The eastern Christians, both those in Virginia and North Carolina under the leadership of James O'Kelly and William Guirey, and those in the New England States led by Abner Jones and Elias Smith, insisted upon the autonomy of the local congregation. Smith opposed associations of churches and missionary societies, believing that all such organizations were contrary to the New Testament.

The Springfield Presbytery, having determined that the New Testament was to be their only standard, "soon found that there was neither precept nor example in the New Testament for such confederacies as modern Church Sessions, Presbyteries, Synods, General Assemblies, etc." They were convinced that consistency of profession and practice necessitated the following item in their will: "We *will*, that our power of making laws for the government of the church, and executing them by delegated authority, forever cease."[1]

In 1813 the Brush Run Church, holding the New Testament as the perfect "constitution for the worship, discipline and government of the New Testament Church," and so stated in the *Declaration and Address*, was accepted into the Redstone Baptist Association as an independent congregation, over the protest of some of its members. The Mahoning Baptist Association of Ohio, influenced by Walter Scott, disbanded in 1830, but continued its fellowship through an annual meeting of Christians having no status as "an advisory council" or "ecclesiastical tribunal."

Another restoration movement, independent of the Stone and Campbell movements in its origin, affected the Free-Will Baptists, Dunkards, Newlights, and Regular Baptists in southern Indiana.

John Wright was responsible for the Blue River Baptist Association disbanding about 1821. Joseph Hostetler contributed to the death of a Dunkard Association about 1828. The preaching of Absalom and John T. Littell, who had adopted reform principles, so upset the churches of the Silver Creek Baptist Association that in 1837 it ceased to meet as an association.

In Kentucky a similar religious revolution was taking place among the Baptists. One example of this religious upheaval may be found in the action of the North District Baptist Association. Greatly influenced by the eccentric and powerful preacher, Raccoon John Smith, the North District Association concluded that there was no authority in the Word of God for this Association to meet at all.[2]

Alexander Campbell began the publication of the *Christian Baptist* in 1823. The opening article of this new periodical was entitled "The Christian Religion." In discussing the life and organization of the early church Mr. Campbell states:

The *order* of their assemblies was uniformly the same. It did not vary with moons and seasons. . . . Their churches were not fractured into missionary societies, Bible societies, Education societies; nor did they dream of organizing such in the world. . . . They knew nothing of the hobbies of modern times. In their church capacity alone they moved. They neither transformed themselves into any other kind of association, nor did they fracture and sever themselves into divers societies. They viewed the church of Jesus Christ as the scheme of Heaven to ameliorate the world; as members of it, they considered themselves bound to do all they could for the glory of God and the good of men. They dare not transfer to a missionary society, or bible society, or education society, a cent or a prayer, lest in so doing they should rob the church of its glory, and exalt the inventions of men above the wisdom of God. In their church capacity alone they moved.[3]

These words were to be urged against Campbell by many of his followers when he began his strong advocacy of co-operation.

CHANGING ATTITUDES

For a time the members of the new movement were too occupied with defending themselves against attacks by leaders of older religious bodies, with arriving at a correct understanding of their own position, and with the proclamation of "simple evangelical Christianity" to give much consideration to the broader aspects of their personal and congregational relationships as parts of the body of Christ.

The movement was composed of a group of self-conscious, autonomous churches, having similarities but also having differences.

The dawning consciousness of a brotherhood with a common task and common responsibilities indicated the need for closer fellowship and co-operation. They were faced with the problem of co-ordinating their efforts for effective service without jeopardizing the freedom of the local congregations. Efforts for co-operation were soon made for purposes of consultation, fellowship, and spreading the gospel.

The eastern Christians began co-operative meetings quite early: Kentucky, 1804; Ohio, 1808; Virginia, 1814; Indiana, 1817; Illinois, New York, Vermont, and Maine, 1818. A United States Christian Conference was organized in 1820.[4]

Alexander Campbell contributed both voice and pen to the growing sentiment favoring responsible co-operation among the churches. He continued to advocate such united efforts despite charges of inconsistency, of reversing his attitude toward extra-congregational associations as set forth in the *Christian Baptist*. In replying to his critics, Campbell insisted that his earlier statements in the *Baptist* had been misunderstood, that they were aimed at the sectarian character of existing organizations; that it was the abuses of such organizations which he opposed; and that the corruption of legitimate means and agencies for the advancement of Christian work in the past history of the church was no valid argument against their rightful use.

In an article entitled "Five Arguments for Church Organization," which appeared in the *Millennial Harbinger* for 1842, Campbell called for "a more rational and scriptural organization."[5] He proposed that organization is essential to Bible distribution, the carrying out of home and foreign missions, the improvement and elevation of the Christian ministry, the protection of the churches from irresponsible preachers, and the best use of the total resources of the church.

Campbell found Scriptural precedent for the co-operation which reason suggested and justified. A group of churches could and must do what the individual congregations found impossible. References in the New Testament to the "Churches in Galatia," the "Churches of Macedonia" and similar expressions, were taken as illustrative of his contention that "the churches were districted in the age of the Apostles." The churches of Galatia and Achaia co-operated in raising money for the poor in Judea; churches united in choosing and appointing persons for certain religious purposes (2 Corinthians 8:19). Those thus chosen, according to Campbell, were "the messengers of the churches" from the districts which chose them. As early as 1831 he proposed a widening circle of co-operation among the churches. Beginning with the county, co-operative organization would ascend through the districts and states to a national level."[6]

EXAMPLES OF EARLY CO-OPERATIVE EFFORTS

The co-operative idea spread rapidly, although not without considerable opposition. It found fertile soil and diligent cultivation in Kentucky, Ohio, Indiana, Illinois, Missouri, Tennessee, Alabama, Virginia, and other states.

As already noted, the Mahoning Baptist Association, infiltrated by restoration concepts, disbanded as an association in 1830, but was continued as an annual meeting. A group estimated at five or six hundred met for three days (Friday through Sunday) at New Lisbon, Ohio, in August, 1831. The time was spent in worship and reports. Walter Scott and Alexander Campbell preached. Eight were immersed. Reports from the preachers present showed about five hundred baptisms during the past year. The matter of co-operation was discussed, resulting in a resolution to co-operate on a county basis. The recommendations were:

These county meetings shall have nothing to do with any church business, of any sort whatever; but shall spend the time in public worship and edification, in hearing reports from the churches, and those who labor in the word, of the success attendant on their operations, and to devise *ways and means* for giving greater publicity to the word in such places as may require their particular attention.[7]

Christians from several counties in Kentucky gathered at Mays Lick in May, 1830, for a general meeting to promote fellowship and co-operation.[8] Matthew Winans reported a co-operation meeting composed of "messengers" from the churches in Clinton and Green counties, Ohio, in the early part of 1835.[9]

The "Eastern District of Virginia and the neighboring counties of Ohio" held a co-operation meeting in Wheeling, March 19, 1836. After listening to reports from the churches, the expediency of co-operation was affirmed. The area was divided into five districts; each was to support an evangelist if possible. It was also recommended that "a general meeting of Messengers from all the churches in co-operation be held annually for mutual information and interchange of sentiments."[10] The report of this meeting was made by Alexander Campbell.

A County Co-operation for Hancock County, Indiana, was held in April, 1836. Peter Roberts and Gabriel M'Duffie were appointed to "ride as evangelists." There were three baptisms during the time of the meeting.[11]

76

Early co-operative efforts in Indiana led to a state meeting in Indianapolis in June, 1839. Education, co-operation, and the sustaining of evangelists were discussed. Reports and statistics of the churches were presented by messengers and letters. The report of this meeting led Campbell to suggest "an annual meeting in some central point of each state in the union, conducted on similar principles, exhibiting the statistics of the churches united in the primitive faith and manners, would in many ways greatly promote the prosperity of the cause." He added, "Co-operation and combination of effort is the great secret of success."[12]

SOCIETIES

The continued emphasis on co-operation eventually led to the organization of societies as the best means or agencies for furthering the interests and work of Christ's kingdom.

American Christian Bible Society

The first society to appeal to the brotherhood for support was the American Christian Bible Society, which was organized in Cincinnati in 1845. The purpose of the society was to "distribute the Sacred Scriptures without notes, or comment." David S. Burnet was elected its first president. The board of managers was made up largely of men from Cincinnati. Alexander Campbell was not present, but was selected as one of nine vice-presidents. He remained somewhat cool toward the society, however, suggesting that it would be better to co-operate with the Baptist Society, the American and Foreign Bible Society, in the distribution of Bibles than to have another society for the same purpose.

A contribution of one dollar per year entitled the contributor to membership; payment of twenty-five dollars constituted a life membership; and one hundred dollars made the donor a life director. Conduct of society affairs was invested in a board of managers consisting of the executive officers and twenty-five members chosen by the society. Reports and an accounting of funds were to be made at the annual meeting of the society in Cincinnati. The constitution also provided for auxiliary societies, with "surplus funds" to be placed in the treasury of the parent society.

American Christian Publication Society

Shortly after the organization of the Bible Society, Christian leaders in Cincinnati launched the Cincinnati Tract Society. Later the name was changed to the Christian Tract and Sunday School Society. In 1851 it became the American Christian Publication Society, publishing the *Christian Age* as its official organ. Efforts to make it the "brotherhood" publishing house failed.

American Christian Missionary Society

Agitation for a more representative co-operative program led to the call for a meeting of messengers or delegates from the churches in Cincinnati (October, 1849). In the August issue of the *Millennial Harbinger,* Campbell stated the importance of such a meeting and described what it should be.

. . . a Convention of messengers of churches, selected and constituted such by the churches—one from every church, if possible, or if impossible, one from a district, or some definite number of churches. It is not to be composed of a few self-appointed messengers, or of messengers from one, two, or three districts, or States, but a *general* Convention. . . .

The purposes . . . a more efficient and Scriptural organization—for a more general and efficient co-operation in the Bible cause, in the Missionary cause, in the Education cause.[13]

Eleven states were represented at this meeting. One hundred and fifty-six delegates represented one hundred churches. The Indiana State Meeting sent delegates. Alexander Campbell was not present, but was elected president. Among the twenty-five vice-presidents, representing fifteen states, were D. S. Burnet, Walter Scott, W. K. Pendleton, John T. Johnson, and Tolbert Fanning.

The new society was to be composed of "annual delegates, Life Members, and Life Directors." An annual contribution of ten dollars entitled a church to one delegate. Life members were those who paid twenty dollars at one time; one hundred dollars made the giver a life director. Duties of an executive board, composed of the duly elected officers, life directors, and twenty-five others elected by the society annually, were:

. . . [to] establish such agencies as the interest of the Society may require, appoint agents and missionaries, fix their compensation, direct and instruct them concerning their particular fields of labors, make all appropriations to be paid out of the Treasury, and present to the Society at each annual meeting a full report of their proceedings during the past year.[14]

According to Article 10, "all the officers, managers, missionaries and agents of the Society, shall be members in good standing of the Churches of God."

The new society recommended the Bible Society to the brotherhood. An organizational pattern consisting of quarterly district meetings and annual state meetings was recommended; the churches were urged to use care in selecting those to be ordained to the ministry; the organization of Sunday schools was encouraged; and a committee of five was appointed to co-operate with the Tract Society in providing Sunday-school books. The first missionary sent out was Dr. James Barclay, who went to Jerusalem in 1851. His stay in this city showed little in the way of tangible results.

While objections continued to be raised about the Scriptural warrant for societies, and especially to the monetary basis of membership and direction, the American Society continued to function until its merger with others in the United Christian Missionary Society. The report of "the mother society" in 1916, shortly before the merger, showed 4,137 churches established; 225,133 baptisms; and $3,040,560.15 disbursed.[15]

Christian Missionary Society

Organization of the Christian Missionary Society was motivated by the abolitionist sentiments of many Disciples. Barclay, the first missionary of the American Society, was a slaveholder. Many felt that a more definite stand needed to be taken on the slavery issue. Unwilling to co-operate in a society where this was ignored, they called a meeting to consider the formation of another society. The name suggested was "Northwestern Christian Missionary Society," but when the meeting convened in Indianapolis in 1859, "Northwestern" was deleted. Pardee Butler was supported as a missionary in Kansas. This society never gained much popularity; the annual receipts seldom exceeded a thousand dollars. The Civil War turned the attention of its advocates to actual conflict, and after the war was over and slavery was abolished by governmental decree, those interested in missions co-operated in the American Society.

Foreign Christian Missionary Society

Dissatisfaction with some aspects of the American Christian Missionary Society, coupled with a desire for some more definite and concentrated efforts in foreign missions, resulted in the organization of the Foreign Christian Missionary Society in 1875, with Isaac Errett as president. Work was carried on in many foreign countries: England, Denmark, France, Turkey, India, Japan, China, Africa, the Philippines. Archibald McLean, as corresponding secretary, did much to "put missions on the map" and popularize the work of the Foreign Society.

Christian Women's Board of Missions

This phase of organized missionary activity began in Cincinnati in 1874. The first president was Mrs. Maria Jameson. Article II stated its object:

. . . to maintain preachers and teachers for religious instruction, to encourage and cultivate a missionary spirit and missionary effort in the Churches, to disseminate missionary intelligence and to secure systematic contributions for such purposes; also, to establish and maintain schools and institutions for the education of both males and females.

The organization of local and state societies was encouraged, each to be subject to the parent society. New life was infused into the missionary work of the churches. Missions were sustained both at home and abroad, and an educational program in mountain areas and among the Negroes was established.

United Christian Missionary Society

Each society and board directed appeals to the churches for the funds needed to carry on their work. The number of these appeals and the competitive struggle for support called for a co-ordination of efforts in the co-operative program, resulting in the creation of the United Christian Missionary Society in 1919. Headquarters, first located in St. Louis, were later moved to Indianapolis. Merging to form the new society were the American Christian Missionary Society, Foreign Christian Missionary Society, Christian Women's Board of Missions, National Benevolent Association, Board of Ministerial Relief, and Board of Church Extension. The official publications of these older organizations were combined in a new organ, *World Call*.

A leadership inclined—at least in many instances—toward liberalism and a changing attitude toward the validity of the plea to restore New Testament Christianity, has tended toward the development of a denominational organization. Criticisms and defences of the United Society have abounded almost from its beginning, primarily involving the development of an ecclesiastical body designed to control and speak for the churches, comity agreements, and the practice of open membership by some of its missionaries.

INTERNATIONAL CONVENTION OF THE CHRISTIAN CHURCHES

The annual meeting of the American Christian Missionary Society, which absorbed the Bible and Tract Societies in 1856, served as a general convention for the Christian brotherhood and became the sounding board for many controversial issues.

The organizational pattern was changed somewhat with the adoption of "The Louisville Plan," which was worked out by a committee of twenty and accepted at the meeting in Louisville in 1869. The changes were designed to facilitate action and to alleviate the criticism that the American Society was representative of individuals and not of the churches.

The "Louisville Plan" involved a delegate system of representation in district, state, and national conventions. The national convention was called the General Christian Missionary Convention. It was to be composed of two delegates from each state, plus one delegate for every five thousand members. Each church was to make its report and present its offering to the district convention, which retained half of the offerings and sent half to the state convention, which, in turn, sent half of the money received to the national organization. Diminished receipts led to appeals for individual gifts in 1873 and a return to a paid membership in 1881.

The national gathering was actually a group of consecutive meetings representing the various societies. The need for a more definitive co-ordinating agency for the work led to the setting up of a "General Convention of Churches of Christ" at Louisville in 1912. The constitution was revised and the name changed to "The International Convention of the Disciples of Christ" in 1917 at Kansas City. The name was again changed in 1956, becoming "The International Convention of the Christian Churches (Disciples of Christ)."

The International Convention was designed to serve both as a delegate convention and a mass meeting of Disciples. All legislation must pass through a Committee on Recommendations, composed of delegates elected by the state conventions, the number of delegates being based on the total membership in the state. This committee presents all matters to the convention, with recommendations for approval or rejection. According to the constitution (but not in actual practice), any missionary, educational, or benevolent agency which submits its annual report to the convention and keeps its books open for inspection may become "a co-operating organization" in the convention, and thus qualifies to make appeals to the brotherhood for continued support.

The International Convention has a secretary, who heads up its work; publishes the *Year Book of the Christian Churches*

(Disciples of Christ); and publishes the reports of those organizations which report to the convention.

Questions

1. What three basic attitudes have been taken toward extra-church organizations such as missionary societies?
2. What did Alexander Campbell have to say about such organizations in 1823? What five arguments did he use to promote organization in 1840?
3. How may free, independent, autonomous churches co-operate?
4. What were the primary purposes of the early "co-operation" meetings?
5. Describe the organization and show the significance of the American Christian Bible Society.
6. Discuss the organization of the American Christian Missionary Society. Name and show the particular purpose of later organizations.
7. What organizations came together to form the United Christian Missionary Society? When?
8. What purpose does the International Convention serve?

Notes

[1]Young, *Historical Documents Advocating Christian Union,* pp. 24, 20.
[2]Williams, *Life of Elder John Smith,* p. 416.
[3]*Christian Baptist,* p. 20; Burnet ed., pp. 6, 7.
[4]M. T. Morrill, *History of the Christian Denomination in America,* pp. 122, 477-479.
[5]*Millennial Harbinger,* 1842, p. 523.
[6]*Ibid.,* 1831, pp. 436-438. See also a series on "The Nature of the Christian Organization" in the *Harbinger* for 1842.
[7]*Ibid.,* 1831, p. 446.
[8]*Ibid.,* 1830, p. 238.
[9]*Ibid.,* 1835, pp. 119, 120.
[10]*Ibid.,* 1836, p. 185.
[11]*Ibid.,* 1836, p. 287.
[12]*Ibid.,* 1839, p. 353.
[14]*Ibid.,* 1849, p. 691.
[15]*Year Book,* 1917.

CHAPTER 9

Some Early Educational Ventures

The "big four" of the Restoration movement in America—Thomas Campbell, Alexander Campbell, Walter Scott, Barton W. Stone—were all well-educated men and teachers, knowing the value of education for themselves and seeking to share its benefits with others.

Thomas Campbell received his early education in a military academy near his home. He was privileged to study at Glasgow University for three years. He later attended the theological school of the Anti-Burgher Seceder Presbyterians for the equivalent of another academic year of study (forty weeks). He taught in southern Ireland for a brief period, then at Sheepbridge, near Newry. In addition to his preaching as a probationer among the Seceders, he taught school at Market Hill. While minister of the church at Ahorey he established an academy in his home at Rich Hill. His career as preacher and teacher continued in America. After his unfortunate experiences with presbytery and synod, he taught near Cambridge, Ohio, at Pittsburgh, Pennsylvania, and Burlington, Kentucky. With his son he taught in Buffalo Seminary.

Alexander Campbell received his early education in an elementary school in Market Hill, in the academy at Newry, conducted by his uncles, Archibald and Enos, and under the personal supervision of his father. One year was spent in study at Glasgow just before coming to America. He was associated with his father in teaching in Ireland and assumed the responsibility for the school at Rich Hill when Thomas Campbell left for America. He was responsible for starting two education institutions in which he taught, Buffalo Seminary and Bethany College.

Walter Scott received his education in Scotland. After preparatory training in an academy he attended the University of Edinburgh. He came to New York in 1818 and almost immediately became a Latin tutor. He joined George Forrester in the school which he was conducting in Pittsburgh. When Forrester drowned, Scott took charge of this school. Later he taught in Mays Lick and Covington, Kentucky. He moved to Steubenville, Ohio, in 1826 to establish an academy. Scott was selected as a trustee of Miami University, Oxford, Ohio, in 1834. When Bacon College was founded in Georgetown, Kentucky, in 1836, Scott was selected as its first president and professor of Hebrew Literature. He was president less than a year, primarily in name only, contributing little to the actual conduct of the school.

Barton Stone received his higher academic training in the school of David Caldwell in North Carolina. He accepted a position at the age of twenty-two in Hope Hull's academy in Washington, Georgia. He later taught in Lexington, Kentucky, and served as principal of Rittenhouse Academy in Georgetown, Kentucky.

Leaders in the Restoration movement have been greatly concerned about education. This concern is shown by the great number of educational institutions that they started. One research worker has compiled a list of more than 250 schools established by those associated with this movement.[1] Others have *estimated* the number at a much higher figure. These schools include institutes, academies, colleges, and seminaries. An emphasis on education for women led to the foundation of a number of academies for women.

BUFFALO SEMINARY

Motivated by the "importance of obtaining the assistance of instructed and cultivated minds in the work to which he was devoted," Alexander Campbell began Buffalo Seminary in his home in 1818. According to Robert Richardson, Campbell had *two* objectives in mind when he established this institution: "He hoped to be able thus not only to confer a benefit upon the neighborhood in giving to the youth a better education than they could otherwise obtain, but also to have the opportunity of preparing some young men for the ministry of the Word."[2]

A number of students came from Pittsburgh, and some from Ohio. Those students living in the immediate neighborhood attended the day classes. Both men and women were accepted. Board and room were provided for $1.50 per week, and tuition was $5.00 per quarter. The curriculum included French and Hebrew. Thomas Campbell assisted his son in the Seminary for some two years after he left Burlington, Kentucky.

Buffalo Seminary continued for four years, 1818-1822. At least three factors were involved in Campbell's decision to close the school: very few of the young men showed any interest in becoming preachers; the close confinement required by his teaching was proving detrimental to his health; and his popularity as a preacher was bringing so many calls for preaching appointments that he could not give the necessary time to the Seminary.

At least two young men from Ohio who studied in this school gave themselves to the ministry. Jacob Osborne, who already had begun preaching, attended the Seminary for two years. He returned to Ohio to preach, but died at Warren in 1839. Joseph Freeman also returned to Ohio to preach reform doctrines among the Baptists. Some of the students attained success in other fields, such as law and medicine.

BACON COLLEGE

Bacon College opened its doors to students in a dwelling house in Georgetown, Kentucky, largely through the efforts of Thornton Johnson, November 14, 1836. Walter Scott became president, at least in name, for about a year. He was succeeded by David S. Burnet. Financial inducements resulted in the college being moved to Harrodsburg in 1839, where, under the direction of Samuel Hatch, sessions were held in a dwelling. James Shannon became president in 1840. He was a well-educated, talented, and conscientious educational leader. Shannon occupied a number of important positions in the educational world, including the presidency of the University of Missouri. Insufficient support led to the suspension of the school in 1850. It was revived in Kentucky University, and Robert Milligan began service as the president of the collegiate department in 1859. The buildings burned in 1864. In 1865 Transylvania University merged with Kentucky University and the school was relocated in Lexington. The Academy and the College of Liberal Arts were continued; a College of Law and a College of the Bible, to educate young men for the ministry, were added.

COLLEGE OF THE BIBLE

This constituent college of Kentucky University, the first Bible college in the Restoration movement, was organized in 1865, with Robert Milligan as president. Milligan and J. W. McGarvey, a graduate of Bethany College, comprised the first faculty. I. B. Grubbs, another Bethany graduate, was added to the faculty later. Because of different concepts of the purpose of the school held by John Bowman, regent of the University, and the faculty of the College of the Bible, particularly J. W. McGarvey, conflicts arose. McGarvey was asked to resign. He refused and was discharged in 1873.

Robert Milligan died in 1875. Robert Graham succeeded to the

85

presidency, and McGarvey was recalled to serve as Professor of Sacred History. When Graham resigned in 1895, McGarvey became president. Under the dynamic leadership of McGarvey and a faculty composed of such men as S. M. Jefferson, Charles Louis Loos, and I. B. Grubbs, the College of the Bible sent forth a stream of young men into the ministry who were faithful to the Word and the principles of the Restoration movement.

With the death of McGarvey in 1911, plans to continue the school on a conservative basis ran into difficulties when R. H. Crossfield was made president of the College of the Bible as well as president of Transylvania. The "old faithful" on the faculty were replaced by such "liberals" as A. W. Fortune, W. C. Bower, G. W. Hemry, and E. E. Snoddy. H. L. Calhoun, who had become dean of the College of the Bible, fought to hold the line, but finally surrendered to the inevitable and resigned. The "liberals" had won the battle and the school.

BETHANY COLLEGE

Nineteen years after the closing of Buffalo Seminary, Alexander Campbell launched a more ambitious educational program. The new institution was chartered as Bethany College in 1840; the first classes were held the following year. According to the charter, Bethany College was to be "a Seminary of learning for the instruction of youth in the various branches of science and literature, the useful arts, agriculture, and the learned and foreign languages."[3]

Campbell donated the land for the campus of Bethany College, gave generously to its establishment, and served as the first president. The areas of teaching assigned to the five men who composed the first faculty were Alexander Campbell, mental philosophy, evidences of Christianity, moral and political economy; A. F. Ross, ancient languages and ancient history; Charles Stewart, algebra and general mathematics; Robert Richardson, chemistry and geology; W. K. Pendleton, natural philosophy and natural sciences.

The student body during the first term numbered about a hundred and fifty. Classes began at 6:30 in the morning and continued until 4:30 in the afternoon. Campbell's morning lectures on the Bible were stimulating, provocative, and challenging. W. T. Moore speaks of the "easy manner, comprehensive sweep, and intense earnestness" which characterized these lectures.[4] The long list of graduates who have been influential in the Restoration movement include Thomas Munnell, Robert Graham, Moses E. Lard, J. W. McGarvey, J. S. Lamar, and Charles Louis Loos. Graduates of

86

Bethany have also attained prominence in politics, law, medicine, and education. Later presidents include W. K. Pendleton, W. H. Woolery, Archibald McLean, Hugh McDiarmid, and B. C. Hagerman.

At the time Bethany College was launched Alexander Campbell declared his purpose to give the remaining years of his life to the development of his particular theory and program of education. His "Plan of a Literary, Moral, and Religious School; or the Union of Four Institutions in one—the combination of the Family, the Primary School, the College, and the Church in one great system of Education" was published in the *Harbinger* for 1839 (pp. 446-451). A more extended discussion of his program is found in a series on "New Institution," which appeared in the *Harbinger* during 1840.

Campbell proposed a four-part program: a preparatory and elementary school for boys 7-14 years of age; an academy of arts and sciences for boys 14 years and older (designed to prepare young men as farmers, mechanics, manufacturers, merchants, etc.); a college, in which a literary and scientific education could be obtained; and a normal school for the preparation of teachers. He proposed a "liberal and comprehensive institution" and stated its purpose:

. . . to model *families, schools, colleges,* and *churches* according to the divine pattern shown to us in the oracles of reason, of sound philosophy, and of divine truth; and to raise up a host of accomplished fathers, teachers of schools, teachers of colleges, teachers of churches, preachers of the gospel, and good and useful citizens, or whatever the church or the state may afterwards choose to make of them.[5]

This educational program was designed to cultivate the physical, intellectual, moral, and social areas of life; but the particular emphasis was on moral education. *"The formation of moral character, the culture of the heart,* is the supreme end of education, or rather is education itself," according to Campbell.[6] All courses were to be developed and taught in the light of this purpose.

The Bible, as "the basis of all true science and true learning," was to be at the center of the educational system. Every mind was to be "enlightened with divine revelation." This applied to those who entered secular fields of service as well as those who desired to preach. Campbell's purpose was not to present a doctrinal system, but to acquaint the student with the Biblical records and spiritual truths. "Bethany College is the only College known to us in the civilized world, founded upon the Bible," Campbell wrote in 1850. "It is not a theological school, founded upon human theology, nor a school of divinity, founded upon the Bible; but a literary and scientific institution, founded upon the Bible as the basis of all true science and true learning."[7]

HIRAM COLLEGE

Hiram College had its beginning as Western Reserve Eclectic Institute at Hiram, Ohio, in 1849; instruction began in 1850. The name was changed to Hiram College in 1867.

The first president was A. S. Hayden. Among the later presidents were James A. Garfield, the only preacher-President of the United States, H. W. Everest, B. A. Hinsdale, and E. V. Zollars. Hinsdale later became the superintendent of schools in Cleveland and a professor of education in the University of Michigan. Zollars, who already had taught in Bethany College and two schools in Kentucky before going to Hiram, later became president of Texas Christian University and Oklahoma Christian University (Phillips University). Isaac Errett suggested the original name and was one of the incorporaters. For a short period beginning in 1865, he was principal and teacher of evangelism, pastoral work, homiletics, and church polity.

Alexander Campbell gave the new school his blessings. Two aspects of the institution may point to the influence of Campbell: a philosophy of education that made the Bible central, and the morning Bible lectures. According to the charter, "the Holy Scriptures shall forever be taught in the institution as the foundation of all true liberty, and of all moral obligation."[8] During Garfield's presidency the morning lectures of the school were not confined to the Bible, but covered a wide range of subjects, including history, morals, education, books, geography, geology, current events.

The first year the school enrolled 313; attendance reached 529 in the 1852-53 academic year.[9] Hayden, in his farewell address, pointed to the fine record and the educational impact of the Institute, both of which he felt compared favorably with any similar institution in the nation. The collegiate division included offerings in the classics, Hebrew, French, and German. According to Hayden, the school "encourages no hothouse scholarship."[10]

Hiram has had a great number of graduates serving with honor and distinction to themselves and to their college in secular and in religious work. Among the latter we find E. B. Wakefield, F. M. Green, Jessie Brown Pounds (the hymn writer), Charles Reign Scoville, W. R. Walker, and P. H. Welshimer.

BUTLER UNIVERSITY

A conviction "by the prominent men among the Christian brotherhood in Indiana, that the prosperity of the Christian cause, as intrusted to their hands, was very intimately blended with the cause of education" led to the discussion of and agitation for the establishment of an institution of higher learning in the Indiana state meetings.[11] The meeting for 1849 voted to establish "Northwestern Christian University" in Indianapolis. A charter was granted in 1850, and a program for selling seventy-five thousand dollars in stocks began immediately.

A preparatory school, under the direction of Allen R. Benton, formerly with Fairview Academy (established in 1843), was opened in the spring of 1855. Buildings were completed, and the university began classes in November of the same year. Like other educational institutions associated with the Restoration movement, the Bible was made a part of the curriculum. The school was coeducational from the beginning. John Young, president, with A. R. Benton and James Challen composed the first faculty. S. K. Hoshour became the second president in 1858, and A. R. Benton the third in 1861.

The college was first located on a campus of twenty acres just beyond the city limits, north of Indianapolis. In 1875 a new campus was obtained and the school moved to Irvington. The name was changed to Butler University in 1877, in honor of Ovid Butler, who had contributed heavily and was closely associated with the school. In 1928 the university moved to Fairview, in north Indianapolis. Originally an institution sponsored by and related to the Christian Churches in Indiana, in later years it has gradually assumed the status of a municipal university.

The School of Religion, a graduate school, was begun in 1925, with Frederick D. Kershner as dean. O. L. Shelton succeeded Kershner as dean. In 1958 the name was changed to Christian Theological Seminary, and it became a separate institution, with Shelton as the first president. A new campus adjacent to the university was purchased. B. A. Norris became president of the Seminary in 1959.

Northwest Christian University did not entirely escape the controversy that surrounded the slavery issue, nor did the school receive the unqualified blessings of Alexander Campbell. When the school was chartered in 1850, Ovid Butler sent a report of the project to Campbell, which was published in the *Millennial Harbinger*. In this communication Butler made the following statement concerning Campbell and Bethany College: "Influenced, it may be, by its local position, as well as by other controlling circumstances, you have apparently, and, we suppose wisely, relied upon the south for its principal support." He closed his letter with an invitation: "We are anxious that you should visit the interior of this State, and especially Indianapolis, but we fear that further importunities would prove as unavailing as the past has been."[12]

Campbell's comments on the project were not particularly friendly. He accused the brethren in Indiana of manifesting a sectional spirit in establishing a "Northwestern" Christian University. As to visiting Indiana, he explained that he often had planned such a tour, but had encountered difficulties which made it impossible for him to visit the state. And by way of further explanation he added: "My tours have been, of necessity, almost universally either in autumn or winter. In autumn, Indiana has been celebrated for fevers, and in winter, for impassible roads."[13]

Campbell denied any sectionalism on his part in beginning Bethany College, either in purpose, location, or name. He warmly defended the position of Bethany in the brotherhood, pointing to its beautiful and healthful location, its well-qualified and experienced faculty, and the splendid record of its graduates. He concluded his reply to Butler with these words:

I hope most satisfactorily to show, what I believe to be capable of satisfactory demonstration, that one good institution, well organized, well furnished with an able cohort of teachers, well patronized by the brethren and the public, is better than ten such as we are likely to have got up and spirited into life by such arguments and efforts, that tend much more to schism, rivalry, and false ambition, than to union, harmony, and successful action. I hope the brethren will hasten leisurely, and hear all the premises and arguments before they act in such a way as to create half-a-dozen of ill-begotten, mishappen, club-footed, imbecile schools, under the name and title of Colleges and Universities. They may strike, but hear me; and if they will only concede a candid hearing, I will give them a candid homily or sermon, either on their own premises or on mine.[14]

OTHER EDUCATIONAL INSTITUTIONS

Limitations of space make it impossible to do more than mention some of the other educational institutions: Milligan College, Eureka College, Culver-Stockton College, Drake University, Chapman College, Texas Christian University, Lynchburg College. These, and many others, may well have received some attention.

The Churches of Christ (non-instrumental) have followed an educational philosophy and policy closely akin to that of Alexander Campbell, and have been responsible for a number of very fine schools and colleges. Among these are Abilene Christian College, Oklahoma Christian College, Florida Christian College, Harding College, Freed-Hardeman College, David Lipscomb College, and George Pepperdine.

Christian Churches and Churches of Christ have also established "Bible Chairs" in a number of universities, including the Universities of Michigan, Virginia, Pennsylvania, and Texas.

In total impact, through specific educational institutions which have been established, and through individual disciples teaching in secular institutions, the Restoration movement has made and still continues to make most significant contributions in the field of education.

Questions

1. What was the educational background of Thomas Campbell, Alexander Campbell, Barton Stone, and Walter Scott?
2. What attitude have leaders in the Restoration movement taken toward education?
3. What two schools did Alexander Campbell start? Why did he start these schools?
4. What particular place was given the Bible in the early schools, such as Bethany, Hiram, and Butler?
5. Name some of the other colleges founded by leaders in the Restoration movement. Who were some of the prominent educators?

Notes

[1]James DeForest Murch, *Christians Only,* p. 200.
[2]Richardson, *Memoirs of Alexander Campbell,* Vol. I, p. 491.
[3]*Millennial Harbinger,* 1840, p. 176.
[4]*Comprehensive History of the Disciples of Christ,* p. 364.
[5]*Millennial Harbinger,* 1839, p. 449.
[6]*Ibid.,* 1840, p. 157.
[7]*Ibid.,* 1850, p. 291.
[8]A. S. Hayden, *Early History of the Disciples in the Western Reserve,* p. 264.
[9]F. M. Green, *Hiram College and Western Reserve Eclectic Institute,* p. 51.
[10]*Ibid.,* p. 92.
[11]Madison Evans, *Biographical Sketches of the Pioneer Preachers of Indiana,* p. 414.
[12]*Millennial Harbinger,* 1850, pp. 330, 331.
[13]*Ibid.,* pp. 332, 333.
[14]*Ibid.,* p. 335.

CHAPTER 10

Periodicals in the
Restoration Movement

"The tongue of the eloquent orator and the pen of the ready writer are the two most potent instrumentalities of moral good or moral evil in the world"—Alexander Campbell.[1]

EDITORS AND THE RESTORATION MOVEMENT

The place of the editor was and is very important in a reformatory movement such as the one under consideration. This was especially true in the earlier, formative years. Each editor determined the character of the periodical for which he sought the public favor and support. He established its purpose and policy. Through personal contributions and articles from the pens of others, he set the tone and fulfilled the destiny of his paper.

Each editor also created a constituency substantially in agreement with the particular emphases of his publication; and, in turn, this constituency supported the paper. While it may be true that some subscribe to a periodical with which they are not in agreement simply because they "want to know what is going on," most people take a paper because it gives them what they want. Cancellations are the strongest protests against changes in editorial policies.

Most of the earlier editors were self-appointed. It must be remembered that in the Restoration movement there has been no agency for controlling the periodical press, no individual or ecclesiastical body having authority to say to one man "You can edit" and to another "You cannot edit." So, while in a sense representing the movement, editors spoke only for themselves.

As early as 1839 Alexander Campbell expressed concern about the number of papers and the choice of editors. "How much the cause we have espoused has suffered by young and inexperienced men assuming the responsibilities of preachers and editors *on their own motion,* is not for me nor any one else to say," he wrote; "but that it has suffered much injury from such hands I am as fully persuaded as I am of the truth of the gospel."[2]

In 1852 he became more outspoken in his criticism of the "voluntary, and only partially educated scribes and irresponsible editors" in the Restoration movement.[3]

The unlicensed press of the present day, and especially in our department of reformation, is the most fearful omen in my horizon. . . .

As a community we have been the most reckless in choosing our editors, our scribes, our elders and our preachers. . . .

We have had a brood of periodicals the most voluntary and irresponsible that I have ever known.[4]

PERIODICALS AND THE RESTORATION MOVEMENT

Positive Contributions

General religious information was included in periodicals on a limited scale. The activities of the religious bodies of the day received some attention from editors, particularly where such events had significance for or bearing on the message of the Restoration movement. *Devotional articles* were published as an aid in developing devotional life and stimulating spiritual growth. *Exposition of the Scriptures* was a major concern of editors, for a knowledge of the Word was vital to a program dedicated to the restoration of New Testament Christianity. *Dissemination of news*—such as the reports of evangelists, successes in local congregations, establishment of new churches, periodicals, educational and benevolent institutions, and announcements and minutes of co-operation meetings—was an important function of periodicals. *Propaganda for the Restoration movement* was found in the periodicals. The principles of the movement were stated and explained, attacks were repelled, misrepresentations pointed out and the truth revealed, and misunderstandings clarified. *Errors in the interpretation of the Bible* were refuted and the "errorists" rebuked.

Negative Contributions

The statement and propagation of speculations and opinions were made possible by editorial freedom. *Partyism* developed and "camps" grew up within the movement, each having its own periodical standard and authority. *Intolerance and dogmatism* were fostered, in some cases at least, by self-appointed judges bent on exposing the errors of others. *Liberty of opinion was denied*, and every matter, however small or insignificant, became an issue fraught with vital and eternal significance. *Crystallization of thought and vocabulary* led to stagnation and enforced immobility. *Editorial jealousy and envy* minimized personal faults and magnified the faults of others. *Love and forbearance often died* in the heat of the various controversies.

HOW MANY PERIODICALS?

This is a question no one has been able to answer satisfactorily. Many have desired to occupy the editorial chair. Two motives have contributed to this desire, service for the Lord and the glory attached to the office and name of editor. There are three ways to limit the number of periodicals: voluntary restraint on the part of would-be editors, mergers of existing periodicals, and lack of support. Perhaps the last has been most significant. A great number of the early periodicals lasted only a short time, being eliminated by the economic sword, the subscribers failing to pay or discontinuing their subscriptions. Alexander Campbell described the editing of a periodical as "a benevolent enterprise."

In 1839 Campbell spoke out against the "periodical zeal" being manifested in the Restoration movement. His arguments against the multiplicity of papers centered in the poor stewardship involved: poor stewardship of time—too much time being spent in editorial duties which could be used to greater advantage in evangelism; poor stewardship of money—a few periodicals well supported was better than many struggling for existence; poor stewardship of the truth—there was a tendency to confuse through many voices and through errors involved in the *new* idea which each editor felt impelled to give his readers.[5]

At this time (1839) Campbell advocated two papers: "a Monthly Quarterly Review, and a large Weekly News-Letter." When he again approached the problem in 1852 he suggested three papers, "one weekly, one monthly and one quarterly." The weekly would be a newssheet, the monthly devoted to fuller discussions of important issues, and the quarterly given over to scholarly matters. Such a program, he said, "would save the community many thousands of dollars per annum for better purposes than for the reading of diluted ideas in Homeopathic doses, as we now have them dispensed in invisible pills, in the ratio of one to a gallon of water."[6] But even Mr. Campbell had little success in persuading men to forego the editorial chair or forsake the editorial fraternity.

SOME RESTORATION PERIODICALS

The earlier publications of the Restoration movement were monthlies. W. W. Eaton sent forth *The Sower* weekly from Pittsburgh in 1854; Benjamin Franklin began the weekly appearance of his *American Christian Review* in 1858; and Elijah Goodwin issued the *Weekly Christian Record* beginning in 1862; other weeklies soon followed. There have been few quarterlies in the Restoration movement, and these few have had a comparatively short life span.

Christian Baptist (Monthly, 1823-1830)

This publication was said to be "the periodical which produced the greatest revolution in thought in this century."[7]

The *Christian Baptist* was a small monthly, the issues of one year making a bound volume of some three hundred pages and measuring about four and one-quarter by seven inches, begun by Alexander Campbell in 1823. During the years of its publication the editor was a Baptist, and the paper, at the suggestion of Walter Scott, went out under the Baptist banner. However, the work itself was an independent journal devoted to a search for Biblical truth. No one could say that the editor failed to fulfill the promise he made in the prospectus for the *Baptist*: "The 'CHRISTIAN BAPTIST' shall espouse no religious sect, except the Ancient Sect, called 'CHRISTIANS FIRST AT ANTIOCH.' Its sole object shall be the eviction of truth, and the exposure of error in doctrine and practice."

The principles of the Campbellian reform movement, which had been incorporated in the *Declaration and Address*, were again given to the public in the *Christian Baptist*, amplified and ably defended. The significant series, "A Restoration of the Ancient Order of Things," which began in volume two and continued through the remaining volumes, included discussions of the Restoration principle, creeds, nomenclature, order of worship, Lord's Supper, fellowship, washing of feet, elders, deacons, singing, discipline. The series on the dispensations in volumes six and seven emphasized the dispensational divisions of the Bible, making distinctions which were so vital and necessary to "rightly divide" the Scriptures.

The *Christian Baptist* was the lash with which Campbell gave the clergy their "forty stripes save one"—most of the time they received their full forty stripes! His "Sermon on Goats," a satire on the clergy, appeared in the first issue. It was followed by a series on "The Clergy," and the ironical "Third Epistle of Peter." Creeds also received considerable editorial attention. Two articles in the series on "Restoration of the Ancient Order" deals with creeds. The "Parable of the Iron Bedstead" pointed to the inconsistency and tyranny of creeds with inescapable logic.

The vitriolic character of the *Baptist* is often referred to. The editor tells us that the tone of the *Baptist* was so by predetermined policy. Efforts of his father at reformation had met with little success. The irenic *Declaration and Address* had made little stir in the religious world. Convinced that "desperate diseases require desperate remedies," Campbell launched the *Christian Baptist*, the first volume of which he describes as "the 'most uncharitable,' the most severe, sarcastic, and ironical he ever wrote." According to the editor, "it was an experiment to ascertain whether society could be moved by fear or rage—whether it could be made to feel at all the decisive symptoms of the mortal malady which was consuming the last spark of moral life and motion."[8]

It would be difficult to overestimate the place of the *Christian Baptist* in the Restoration movement. Through this paper such men as Joseph Hostetler in southern Indiana, John P. Thompson in eastern Indiana, Chester Bullard in Virginia, and countless other men were led to a deeper understanding of and great efforts for restoring New Testament Christianity. Later, the words of this periodical were to become a wedge, separating brethren on the validity of co-operation in such projects as missionary societies and Christian colleges.

When the *Christian Baptist* began, Alexander Campbell was a popular and influential young Baptist preacher, having just successfully defended the Baptist cause in a debate with John Walker and preparing for his encounter with another Presbyterian, W. L. MacCalla. When it closed, the Baptists had contributed hundreds of members, including entire congregations and associations, to the Restoration movement, and all "Campbellites" were being expelled from the Baptist fellowship as rapidly as possible.

Christian Messenger (Monthly, 1826-1845)

The *Christian Messenger*, comparable with the *Christian Baptist* in size and make-up, was first published at Georgetown, Kentucky, and later at Jacksonville, Illinois, when Stone moved there in 1834. This periodical is irenic in tone, breathing some of the gentleness, tenderness, and warmth of the "apostle of unity." It contributed greatly to Stone's leadership among the western Christians.

Christian unity, which Stone says he took as his "polar star," is a recurring topic in the *Messenger*. The editor began a series on union in the first issue. At the time of the union between the Reformers and Christians in 1832, Stone took John T. Johnson, Reformer, to labor with him in promoting union between the two bodies.

The *Messenger* was opposed to slavery. The anti-slavery senti-ments of the editor revealed in the periodical, including some articles on this vexing problem copied from the *Harbinger,* caused many in the south to cancel their subscriptions.[9] Stone had owned some slaves at one time, but had given them their freedom.

Here, too, Stone discussed various theological concepts, including election and predestination, the Trinity, and the atonement. His unorthodox views of the Trinity and the atonement, particularly the latter, led to extended discussions with the Campbells, and made many of the Reformers somewhat reluctant to freely accord Stone and his followers full fellowship.

Millennial Harbinger (Monthly, 1830-1870)

The *Millennial Harbinger* was somewhat larger in size and expanded in number of pages, compared with the *Christian Baptist*. Under the militant editorial policy of Alexander Campbell, the *Harbinger* was the dominant voice in the Restoration movement for many years. W. K. Pendleton was its editor from 1865-1870.

The change from the *Christian Baptist* to the *Millennial Harbinger* was due, in part at least, to the actions of the Baptists against Campbell and those associated with him. Campbell had determined to remain with the Baptists just as long as they would tolerate his independent New Testament position; the point of "no toleration" had been reached. By 1830 those opposed to him had succeeded in having "Campbellism" anathematized in many local congregations and Baptist associations, so that the editor of the *Christian Baptist* was not welcome in their churches or associational meetings. The paper had fulfilled its mission; there was no longer any need for maintaining the name "Baptist" in his editorial labors. A new era was beginning; a new paper with a new name was called for.

Essays, Biblical expositions, discussions, news—these formed the major portion of each issue. The exposition and defense of the basic principles of the Restoration movement were continued in the *Harbinger*. During the first decade the editor published a number of "extras," which were essays on such matters as remission of sins, regeneration, kingdom of heaven, education, order, and the loaf. These were later put together in a volume having the binder's title *Christianity Restored*; still later they appeared as *The Christian System*.

In the *Harbinger* Campbell reveals a growing interest in bring-ing order to a group of independent churches having both likenesses and differences, which were jealous of their congregational liberty. When the editor campaigned in behalf of co-operation and united brotherhood action, and cast his vote for co-operative agencies as legitimate means through which the church could function, the course of the movement in such areas was practically decided.

Why did Campbell choose the name *Millennial Harbinger* for his new paper? He was convinced that a successful restoration of Biblical Christianity would usher in the millennium.[10] In 1840 he wrote, "When we put to sea under this banner we had the port of Primitive Christianity, in letter and in spirit, in profession and practice, in our eye; reasoning that all the Millennium we could scripturally expect was not merely the restoration of the Jerusalem church in all its moral and religious character, but the extension of it through all nations and languages for one thousand years."[11] In keeping with this view, Campbell worked for the annihilation of partyism, restoration of pure speech, preaching of the original gospel, restoration of the Christian ordinances, and the reception of larger measures of the Holy Spirit.

American Christian Review (Monthly and Weekly, 1856-)

Benjamin Franklin, who had published a monthly periodical for a number of years under the names *Reformer, Proclamation and Reformer,* and *Western Reformer,* began the *American Christian Review* in Cincinnati in 1856. For two years it was published as a monthly and then was changed to a weekly. Daniel Sommer became the editor when he bought the paper from Franklin. Sommer changed the name to *Octographic Review* and later to *Apostolic Review.* It is currently published in Indianapolis as the *American Christian Review,* the editors having returned to the original name.

Franklin and his periodicals lack the polish manifested in some of the other papers, yet they do not suffer greatly by comparison. He had little formal education. His writing was simple and clear; his readers certainly could understand his meaning. He was sincere, straightforward, and thoroughly committed to Restoration ideals. Franklin wielded great influence, both as a preacher and as an editor.

The editor of the *Review* vascillated for a time when the agitation for societies was strong. He was present in Cincinnati when the American Christian Missionary Society was formed and he co-operated in the work. He served as corresponding secretary with C. L. Loos in 1857. He helped to establish the short-lived

American Christian Publication Society in 1851. For a time he rejoiced over the adoption of "The Louisville Plan" and its provisions for church representation in the co-operative program. But he later became the foe of the organized pattern for church co-operation. He also threw the weight of the *Review,* often referred to as "The Old Reliable," against the use of instrumental music in worship and contributed to the division over this issue.

Christian Standard (Weekly, 1866-   )

Dissatisfaction with the growing legalistic attitude in the Restoration movement, especially as expressed by the *American Christian Review,* led to the formation of the Christian Publishing Association, a joint stock company chartered January 2, 1866, which immediately called Isaac Errett to become the editor of a new periodical, the *Christian Standard.* The office was first located in Cleveland, but was later moved to Cincinnati. The first issue, dated April 7, 1866, carried an obituary of Alexander Campbell. Purchase of the *Weekly Christian Record,* published in Indianapolis by Elijah Goodwin, provided a nucleus of some two thousand subscribers. Financial difficulties led the directors to turn the company and the *Standard* over to Errett within two years.

Errett committed the *Standard* to a policy that made it an outstanding religious journal: a bold and vigorous advocacy of New Testament Christianity; emphasis on the plea for union; challenge to practical piety; support of worthy missionary, educational, and benevolent institutions; review of Christian literature, education, moral and political 'science, and commerce; analysis of important religious movements in America and elsewhere, with particular emphasis upon their significance for the message and mission of the Restoration movement.[12]

The new paper was to be "Scriptural in aim, catholic in spirit, bold and uncompromising, but courteous in tone." It would "seek to rally the hosts of spiritual Israel around the Bible for the defense of truly Christian interests against the assumption of popery, the mischiefs of sectarianism, the sophistries of infidelity, and the pride and corruption of the world."[13]

If the editor of the *Millennial Harbinger* had a successor, his mantle fell on Isaac Errett. He had served for two years on the staff of the *Harbinger.* His first series of articles on "A Plea for Reformation," which appeared in the *Harbinger* during 1861, revealed the same analytical ability, grasp of essentials, and breadth of treatment which marked the writing of Alexander Campbell.

99

His later work continued to manifest the same spirit and ability.

While Errett joined those favoring missionary societies and instrumental music, he refused to make these tests of fellowship, pleading for understanding and forbearance where differences prevailed. Later the *Standard* opposed the rising tide of liberalism in education. J. W. McGarvey's ably conducted department of "Biblical Criticism" was both an answer to destructive criticism and an apologetic for Biblical trustworthiness. The *Standard* also has publicized and opposed the practical repudiation of the plea of the Restoration movement manifested in the development of ecclesiastical concepts and practices in conventions and missionary societies, and the practice of open membership in local congregations and on the mission fields.

Gospel Advocate (Weekly, 1855-   )

The *Gospel Advocate* was begun by Tolbert Fanning and William Lipscomb in 1855. Except for a short period when it was suspended during the Civil War, it has continued to the present. David Lipscomb and E. G. Sewell are among its distinguished editors; B. C. Goodpasture is the present editor. From its beginning the *Advocate* has opposed "innovations" in the work of the church, including the use of instrumental music in worship. It has become more liberal in its attitudes toward missionary and benevolent enterprises, and has favored the fine educational system promoted by the Churches of Christ.

The Christian (Formerly, Christian-Evangelist; weekly, 1882-   )

Genealogy of the *Christian* is often traced through editorial succession to the *Christian Messenger* of Barton Stone. The *Christian,* edited by J. H. Garrison in St. Louis, and the *Evangelist,* edited by B. W. Johnson in Chicago, united in October, 1882, to form the *Christian-Evangelist.*

During the lifetime of Garrison and Errett the *Christian-Evangelist* and the *Christian Standard* were somewhat similar in tone and emphases. Divergencies began following the death of Errett. The *Standard* has continued in a conservative direction, while the *Christian,* particularly in recent years, has been inclined toward a more liberal reinterpretation of the principles held by the early reformers. As "The Brotherhood Paper," it has been more and more closely identified with the agencies of the Disciples and with interdenominational organizations.

Quarterlies

Lard's Quarterly (1863-1868) is filled with the editor's vigorous, and often bitter, "anti" sentiments, especially in his opposition to instruments in worship. The *Christian Quarterly* (1869-1876) was marked by a broader and less strict interpretation of the principles of the Restoration movement. It was a scholarly journal. Under the able editorship of W. T. Moore it was recognized as an outstanding religious periodical, both in America and Europe. The *New Christian Quarterly* (1892-1899) was edited by J. H. Garrison and W. T. Moore. In character and policy it resembles the older *Christian Quarterly*.

Questions

1. How have men been chosen to serve as editors in the Restoration movement?
2. What factors were involved in a man continuing as an editor?
3. How have periodicals served to advance the principles and objectives of the Restoration movement?
4. In what ways have periodicals hindered this movement?
5. Characterize and show the importance of the following periodicals: *Christian Baptist, Millennial Harbinger, American Christian Review, Christian Standard, The Christian.*
6. How may periodicals best serve the local congregation?

Notes

[1]*Millennial Harbinger,* 1852, p. 390.
[2]*Ibid.,* 1839, p. 550.
[3]*Ibid.,* 1852, p. 494.
[4]*Ibid.,* 1852, pp. 390, 391.
[5]*Ibid.,* 1839, p. 550.
[6]*Ibid.,* 1852, p. 391.
[7]Baxter, *Life of Elder Walter Scott,* p. 73.
[8]*Millennial Harbinger,* 1831, pp. 419, 420.
[9]Cf. *Christian Messenger,* 1832, p. 223.
[10]Cf. *Christian Baptist,* Burnet edition, p. 128.
[11]*Millennial Harbinger,* 1840, p. 561.
[12]J. S. Lamar, *Memoirs of Isaac Errett,* Vol. I, pp. 305, 306.
[13]*Ibid.,* p. 306.

CHAPTER 11

Twentieth Century Developments—I

A number of issues disturbed the peace and impeded the progress of the Restoration movement. Three of the most significant of these have been instrumental music, liberalism, and open membership.

INSTRUMENTAL MUSIC

Cause for Division

Should instrumental music be permitted in the worship of Christians? This issue was brought into the Restoration movement at a comparatively early period, but did not receive too much attention until the latter half of the nineteenth century. Although the controversy arose during the closing years of the nineteenth century, it bore its bitter fruit of division in the early dawn of the twentieth. The tragedy of division in a movement committed to unity was formally recognized in the United States Religious Census for 1906. In that year those churches using the instrument were listed as "Disciples of Christ," and those rejecting its use as "Churches of Christ."

The use of an instrument in worship was discussed widely and earnestly, quite often with unrestrained emotion and bitter feeling. In reading the literature produced by this controversy one finds it difficult to escape the conclusion that much of the discussion and debate has been concerned with maintaining a position rather than searching for the truth. Alexander Campbell wrote in 1851: "To all spiritually-minded Christians, such aids would be as a cow bell in a concert."[1] Moses E. Lard, one of the most determined opponents of instrumental music in worship, writes of those who "contemn the authority of Christ by resorting to will worship," suggesting that it would be better to "live out of a church than go into such a den" where there was an instrument.[2]

Beliefs of Opposing Sides

Those favoring the use of the instrument offered the following justification for this practice: it is expedient; there is no prohibition

102

of its use in the New Testament; it has Scriptural sanction through its use in the worship of God by the Jews and in the worship of God in heaven (Revelation 5:8,9; 14:2,3); it violates no teaching or command of Christ or His apostles; it does not void the command to sing, but is merely an aid to singing.

Those who opposed the use of the instrument argued: it is an "innovation"; there is no evidence of its use in apostolic times; the Scriptures enjoin singing, but give no command to *play and sing*; without "express command" or "approved precedent" it can have no place in the worship of Christians.

Basically, these arguments involved two different attitudes toward the *silences* of the Scriptures. Is Scriptural silence equivalent to prohibition? The opponents of instrumental music said yes. Moses Lard writes: "In all acts of worship we must do *only* what is prescribed in the New Testament, or was done with divine sanction by the primitive Christians."[3]

On the other hand, there were those who believed that Scriptural silence involved the "law" of freedom. "I must still contend, therefore," wrote J. S. Lamar, "that 'within the Word is authority—all beyond is liberty.' "[4]

Later, O. E. Payne, in a work entitled *Instrumental Music Is Scriptural* (*Standard Publishing Company*, 1920), approached the problem through an examination of the Greek word *psallo*. In his study of Greek lexicons Payne found that the root meaning of the word was "to pluck, as the strings of an instrument," and that it was the word used by a writer when he wished to indicate singing with an instrument.

In recent years the argument that every *element* of worship is prescribed in the New Testament, and to use an instrument is to introduce *a foreign element* into worship, has received some attention. Those using the instrument have called for the Scripture which establishes *singing* as an *element of worship*. If the list given in Acts 2:42 is a list of such elements, then singing is not included. Furthermore, the two passages most often cited by opponents of instrumental music, Ephesians 5:19 and Colossians 3:16, have no reference to *public worship* and must be taken out of their context of *personal admonitions* to make them apply to such worship.

Hopes for Reconciliation

Through the years some continued to hope that a restoration of fellowship between these divergent groups was possible. In recent years some definite steps have been taken in an attempt to realize these hopes. Under the direction of James DeForest Murch (instrumental) and Claude Witty (non-instrumental) representatives of both groups came together in Cincinnati in 1937 to discuss the situation. Other meetings were held later in different parts of the nation.

These exploratory conferences were designed to get the leaders acquainted with each other; to establish some basis for fellowship, even on a limited scale; to find areas of agreement; to discuss areas of disagreement as Christians concerned about the division; and to pray for unity. A National Unity Meeting was held in Detroit in 1938 and another in Indianapolis the following year. Witty and Murch began publishing the *Christian Unity Quarterly* (later, *Unity Quarterly*) in April, 1943, to further the efforts for unity. After about ten years a number of factors combined to discourage these particular efforts for unity.

However, efforts to do something about the situation did not cease entirely. In 1950 Ernest Beam, a minister of the Church of Christ, but who refused to limit fellowship by the use of an instrument, began the *Christian Forum,* a periodical designed to destroy partyism and promote fellowship with the instrumental brethren. Carl Ketcherside, editor of the *Mission Messenger,* has led in a significant movement, promoting "brotherhood" meetings in an attempt to emphasize the *basic* areas in which fellowship lies and to approach the problem with sympathetic understanding.

LIBERALISM

Development

Liberalism is a rationalistic, humanistic philosophy that attained prominence during the latter half of the nineteenth century, becoming particularly prevalent in America during the first half of the twentieth century (1900-1935). Its rise and development was influenced by the modern scientific method, the evolutionary theory of Charles Darwin, the philosophies of Kant and Hegel, and the historical-critical approach to the study of the Bible. Liberalism vitally affected every area of Christian emphasis. Liberals challenged the traditional faith of evangelical Christians, including their concepts of the Bible, God, Christ, man, sin, the church, salvation, immortality, heaven, and hell.

Christianity was assigned a place as one of many religions, similar to and comparable with the other religions in many respects, having no particularly unique or revelatory character.

104

Biblical inspiration, in any real meaning of inspiration, was denied. The Bible had validity for the people of its day only; its primary value for the modern day is historical rather than normative, a document showing one phase of man's religious development and illustrative of the evolutionary process, by which man is inclined ever upward in the scale of life. Miracles mentioned in the Bible were attributed to natural causes or otherwise explained away.

God was considered an immanent force in the world, a view of God which, in some instances at least, was difficult to distinguish from pantheism. The Jehovah of the Hebrews was merely a tribal deity.

Christ was not the divine Son of God. There was a Jesus of history, but no supernatural Christ. This Jesus was the natural development of the ages; a good man, a prophet, the exponent of splendid ethical concepts, but not divine.

The church is an evolutionary development, having no fixed doctrine or laws. It must be changed and adapted to meet the needs of every age. There can be no "going back"; it must be ever "onward, forward."

Man was exalted in proportion as God was minimized. The rejection of Biblical authority was followed by the establishment of human experience as the authoritative standard for life. The development of the "social gospel" followed.

The Christ of the cross has no redemptive significance for the world, only ethical significance. Salvation is reformation. Man needs no "sacrifice" for his sins, he merely needs to be challenged to bring out the good inherent in everyone. All men are potentially divine, not because of something God does for them, but because of what they can do for themselves.

Since nothing concerning the hereafter can be verified through experience or scientific investigation, then nothing positive can be said concerning heaven, hell, or the ultimate destiny of man.

Introduction to Colleges and Universities

Liberalism was introduced into the colleges and universities of America, heralded as the new approach to the understanding of man and his religion. Of particular significance for the Restoration movement was the capture of Yale University by the liberals and the commitment of the University of Chicago (organized in 1892) to the "new learning." Many of the ministers and other leaders of the Christian churches were educated in these two institutions and were thoroughly indoctrinated in the tenets of liberalism.

A number of related factors—in time, emphasis, and purpose—contributed to the spread of liberalism in the Restoration movement. The Disciples Divinity House was established at the University of Chicago, with Herbert L. Willett as dean, in 1894. The Campbell Institute was organized in 1896. Herbert L. Willett, Burris Jenkins, and E. S. Ames were among the incorporaters. The *Christian Oracle* was purchased in 1901 and later became the *Christian Century.* A series of Congresses (1899-1926) were set up to discuss problems pertinent to the brotherhood.

The leaders of these various enterprises were college men committed to keeping the "scholarly spirit" alive, to being "sympathetically" aware of developments in the new approach to man and Christianity. The *Bulletin* of the Campbell Institute became the *Scroll.* The *Scroll* and the *Christian Century,* which was purchased by C. C. Morrison in 1908, became propaganda sheets for liberalism and open membership. The Congresses of the Disciples publicized the new doctrines and brought them into wider acceptance. They were so completely dominated by members of the Campbell Institute that the conservatives soon ceased to participate in them.

The schools of the Disciples were soon infiltrated by men holding the new theology. One by one, with hardly an exception, the old order was superseded by the new. For example, the College of the Bible, long a bulwark of faith under the direction of men thoroughly committed to New Testament Christianity, fell to the liberals. Ministers and leaders trained in the new atmosphere carried its conclusions and emphases into the churches and the missionary societies.

Effect of Liberalism Upon Restoration Movement

The controversy caused by a leadership committed to liberalism has been a major factor in at least two developments in the Restoration movement: a division into two "camps," liberals and conservatives, having little love and little or no fellowship, and the creation of a new educational institution designed to provide a Biblically sound leadership for the churches, the Bible college.

OPEN MEMBERSHIP

"Open membership" is the reception of the "pious unimmersed" who transfer membership into a local congregation without being required to be immersed. Immersion may still be, and usually is, required of all "non-Christians" for church membership.

Immersion the Common Practice

The Brush Run Church gave no consideration to baptismal requirements for membership at the time of its organization. Within a few months, however, the practice of immersion was adopted and required for membership. It was on this basis—they were "baptists"—that the congregation and its ministers were welcomed into the Redstone Baptist Association.

Under the influence of Alexander Campbell, Walter Scott, and, to some extent at least, Barton Stone, immersion "for the remission of sins" (Acts 2:38; 22:16) was the practice of the preachers and churches associated in the Restoration movement. Immersion, preceded by faith, repentance, and confession, was required for church membership; even the "pious unimmersed" transferring membership from other religious groups were immersed. Those of the Kentucky Christians who united with the Reformers beginning in 1832 followed the same practice.

The Lunenburg Letter

This letter, written by a "conscientious sister" from Lunenburg, Virginia, was published in the *Millennial Harbinger* for 1837, accompanied by the editor's discussion of the issue it raised. The concluding question of this brief letter was: "Does the name of Christ or Christian belong to any but those who believe the *gospel,* repent, and are buried by baptism into the death of Christ?"[5]

Campbell's reply involved him in considerable controversy with many of his brethren. It is frequently quoted by advocates of open membership in support of this practice. It seems difficult to reconcile some statements in his discussion at the time and in later articles. For example, note these two statements:

Who is a Christian? I answer, Every one that believes in his heart that Jesus of Nazareth is the Messiah, the Son of God; repents of his sins, and obeys him in all things according to his measure of knowledge of his will.

. . . .

He only has praise of God and man, and of himself *as a* Christian, who believes, repents, is baptized, and keeps all the ordinances, positive and moral, as delivered to us by the holy Apostles.[6]

According to Mr. Campbell, there are "Christians" who have not been immersed—imperfect Christians. Some have an imperfect knowledge of God's plan; imperfect knowledge leads to imperfect obedience; and imperfect obedience makes an imperfect Christian. He makes a distinction between the Christian *state* and *character*; one may have the latter without the former; he may be an *inward*

Christian without having become an *outward* Christian (through baptism).

Campbell's ultimate answer to his critics was that he had expressed an opinion, adding, "My *opinion* is no rule of action to my brethren."[7] The editor of the *Harbinger* might readily express his *opinion* that there are "Christians among the sects," but he did not advocate admitting the unimmersed into the church. In 1831 he criticized Stone and the Christians for making "immersion of non-effect by receiving persons into the kingdom of Jesus, so called, irrespective of their being legitimately born."[8] And in *The Christian System* he asserts that "all that is required of Heaven for admission into the church"[9] is belief of one fact—Jesus is the Christ—and submission to one institution—baptism.

The Practice of Open Membership

For many years those associated in the Restoration movement practiced immersion and admitted to church membership only those who were immersed. Contemporary with the rise of liberalism, however, was a growing sentiment in favor of open membership.

As early as 1869 L. L. Pinkerton advocated receiving the unimmersed into full fellowship. In 1889 R. L. Cave proposed the abolition of all restrictions on baptism. About five years later Thomas Munnell, a former secretary of the American Christian Missionary Society, suggested open membership as an aid in the promotion of Christian union. Samuel H. Church, grandson of Walter Scott, caused quite an uproar when he advocated open membership in the Centennial Convention at Pittsburgh in 1909.

W. T. Moore, in the *Christian Quarterly* for 1897 and again when speaking before the Congress of the Disciples in 1901, proposed a plan for promoting union. According to this plan, all Christians would come together, forming a united church, disregarding the baptismal issues, but afterward only immersion would be practiced. C. C. Morrison promoted open membership in a series of articles in the *Christian Century* in 1911. Some attempted to meet the problem by receiving the unimmersed into an associate membership.

A. T. DeGroot found nineteen churches *openly* committed to the practice of open membership in 1929.[10] Carl Ledbetter reported 120 churches practicing open membership in 1940.[11] DeGroot, as the result of a second study in 1948, reported about the same number as were found eight years earler, but *estimated* the number committed to the practice either openly or "quietly" at about 500.[12]

Despite denials, there was little question that open membership had been instituted by missionaries with the Foreign Christian Missionary Society and later with the United Christian Missionary Society. Controversy centered first on practices in the China and the Philippine missions. A long and often "bitter" struggle by "conservatives" to bring the practice on the foreign fields into harmony with the practice of the main body of Christians in America through the societies and through the International Convention proved unsuccessful. The result was withdrawal from these co-operative agencies and the inauguration of an "independent" or "direct-support" missionary program.

Questions

1. What was meant by the slogan, "Where the Scriptures speak, we speak; where the Scriptures are silent, we are silent"?
2. How has this slogan been used in the instrumental music controversy?
3. What efforts are being or have been made to heal the division over the use of an instrument in worship?
4. What is liberalism?
5. What basic principle of the Restoration movement does liberalism affect?
6. Through what particular medium has liberalism gone into the churches?
7. What is open membership?
8. How prevalent is the practice of open membership in churches which have been associated in the Restoration movement?

Notes

[1]*Millennial Harbinger,* 1851, p. 582.
[2]*Lard's Quarterly,* 1864, p. 332.
[3]*Ibid.,* 1867, p. 395. Italics are the writer's.
[4]*Millennial Harbinger,* 1868, p. 666.
[5]*Ibid.,* 1837, p. 411.
[6]*Ibid.,* 1837, pp. 411, 508.
[7]*Ibid.,* 1837, p. 508.
[8]*Ibid.,* 1831, p. 392.
[9]*The Christian System,* p. 101.
[10]B. D. Thesis, Butler University.
[11]B. D. Thesis, Butler University, published in the *Christian Standard* during 1940, 1941.
[12]Garrison and De Groot, *The Disciples of Christ,* p. 440.

CHAPTER 12

Twentieth Century Developments—II

The developments discussed in the preceding chapter—instrumental music, liberalism, and open membership—are primarily doctrinal. Two of them, instrumental music and open membership, are involved in congregational practices; but even these are rooted in specific doctrines, worship and baptism. All three reflect significant attitudes toward the Scriptures. Instrumental music is significant of the silences of the Bible; liberalism, the character and authenticity of the Bible as the divinely inspired Word of God; open membership—the purpose and authority of the Bible in governing the practices of the church.

The developments to be considered in this chapter—direct-support missions, North American Christian Convention, Bible colleges, and Christian service camps—are reactions to liberalism and its translation into the faith and practice of the church. At the same time they are objective expressions of deep convictions concerning the necessity for implementing the commission of Jesus to evangelize the world and bring Christians to maturity in Him; and to do everything in keeping with the spirit and teaching of the New Testament.

DIRECT-SUPPORT MISSIONS

Three attitudes toward missionary societies have had adherents in the Restoration movement. The first is that societies are Scriptural, not necessarily as "societies," but as co-operative efforts to advance the Master's kingdom. They have precedent in the association of churches in New Testament times for benevolent and missionary purposes. The second attitude is that societies are anti-Scriptural, being contrary to the program of Christ. He established the church and the church *alone. It* is *the* missionary society; every Christian is a member and functions through *this* society.[1] The third is that societies are non-Scriptural, falling into the category of "expedients," to be established and perpetuated as occasion demands and as they prove useful and effective. They may be supported or not supported at the discretion of every Christian. The establishment of missionary societies as an expression of the co-operative life and missionary endeavor in the Restoration movement has been based on the conviction that such organizations have New Testament precedent, or that they are expedient.

Societies Infiltrated by Liberals

These societies were later infiltrated by liberals, those liberal in their attitudes toward the Scriptures and in the interpretation of the principles of the Restoration movement. The organizational life of the Disciples more and more assumed a denominational character. The status and operation of a denomination were accepted.

Comity agreements were entered into with other denominations. A comity agreement is an arrangement whereby two or more denominations accept boundaries for the area in which they work. Evangelistic, educational, and benevolent efforts are confined within these areas. Weak churches may be closed in communities where another has greater strength. Interdenominational projects, such as educational institutions, may be maintained on a co-operative basis.

While controversy engendered by liberalism and open membership had begun much earlier in the twentieth century, proposals for the union of the China Mission with the liberal "Church of Christ in China" (not the non-instrumental body) in 1920 brought to light the practice of open membership in the China Mission. A battle was waged through the International Convention to force the United Society to recall all missionaries committed to or practicing open membership, but the personnel of the society were able to circumvent every action of the convention.

John T. Brown, a conservative on the board of the newly-organized (1919) United Christian Missionary Society, made a trip to the various missions in an attempt to get the facts concerning the work of foreign missions. His report, indicating the practice of open membership in China and the Philippines, was published in the *Christian Standard* and in a pamphlet entitled *The U.C. M.S. Self-Impeached.*

Society Ignores Resolution

In 1925, at the meeting of the International Convention in Oklahoma City, Z. T. Sweeney introduced a "peace resolution": no individual out of harmony with the historic positions of the Restoration movement, or committed to the practice of open membership, was to be employed by the United Christian Missionary

Society, and all such then employed by the society were to be released. Although the resolution was passed by the convention with a strong majority, leaders of the society, particularly F. W. Burnham, so interpreted the resolution as to ignore and nullify any vital significance or application that it might have. Liberals and advocates of open membership, many of whom had prepared or were ready to prepare their resignations, were retained by the society. Another effort was made at the convention in Memphis in 1926 to induce the society to restore their policies to a sound Biblical basis; it also proved unsuccessful.

Individuals and churches began withdrawing support from the United Society in increasing numbers. These had completely lost confidence in the integrity of leaders who seemed determined to carry out their own policies—policies repudiated by the Disciples as expressed through the International Convention, the only agency through which an "official" expression of their disapproval could be voiced. Some still hoped, and worked from within the society in an attempt to salvage the investment which had been made through the earlier missionary societies.

Periodicals Begin

Three periodicals began in 1925 as a direct result of this controversy. The *Christian Standard,* which had been the principal medium for publicizing the policies of the United Society, began *The Touchstone* (first issued as *The Spotlight*). R. E. Elmore was chosen editor of this publication, which was dedicated to exposing errors in doctrine and practice in the Restoration movement. The United Society's answer and antidote to this periodical was the *United Society News,* edited by W. M. Williams. The Christian Restoration Association was organized in September, 1925. The *Restoration Herald,* with James DeForest Murch as editor, was launched as the organ of this Association and a medium for promoting home and foreign missions, education, and the work of the "associated free agencies" desiring to take advantage of its services.

Direct-support Missions

As early as 1891 Miss Loduska Wirich was operating as an "independent" missionary in Japan. W. K. Azbill began working in Japan about the same time. W. D. Cunningham (Yotsuya Christian Mission), who for physical reasons was rejected for service with the Foreign Christian Missionary Society, began missionary work "on his own" in Japan in 1901. A great number of "independent" missions were organized in the twenties: Mexican Christian Missionary Society (E. T. Westrup), Philippine Mission Church of Christ (Leslie Wolfe), Osaka Christian Mission (M. B. Madden), Christian Mission to India (Dr. S. G. Rothermel), Central Provinces India Mission (Harry Schaeffer), Tibetan Christian Mission (J. Russell Morse).

The number of direct-support missionaries multiplied exceedingly following the twenties. New missions were opened and the list of missionary recruits continued to grow. In spite of disruptions and setbacks occasioned by war, by 1963 the number of foreign missionaries in Africa, Asia, Europe, various islands, Mexico, and South America had grown to 329. Add to this number 170 working in missionary projects in the United States and nine in Canada and we have a total of 508 engaged in missionary activities at home and abroad.[2]

A missionary society, the Christian Missionary Fellowship—proposing "to evangelize the non-Christian people of the world in the order, manner, and fashion of a missionary society"—was incorporated in 1949. In 1957 William L. Thompson was called to serve as the General Administrator, with headquarters in Aurora, Illinois. Mission work has been carried on in Brazil, Japan, and India.

The expanding program in the United States includes missions among the Indians and Negroes, children's homes and homes for the aged, and ten Christian day schools. In addition to local use of radio and television, on a broader scope the Christian's Hour, the Gospel Broadcasting Mission, and Christian Television Mission, which produces "Homestead U.S.A.," are maintained. New church evangelism in metropolitan areas in various sections of the nation is a part of the growing evangelistic emphasis. In the years 1960-1963 approximately two hundred new congregations were established.

NORTH AMERICAN CHRISTIAN CONVENTION

The conduct of the International Convention during its sessions in Memphis in 1926 left many thoroughly disgusted with the deportment of this body. Those who felt that the leaders of the convention and the United Christian Missionary Society were acting in bad faith and out of harmony with the expressed wishes of the great body of the Christian brotherhood, came together to discuss the situation. A Committee on Future Action was selected, consisting of P. H. Welshimer, W. R. Walker, Mark Collis, W. E. Sweeney,

O. A. Trinkle, Robert S. Tuck, and F. S. Dowdy. This committee issued a call for a national gathering of Christians in a "North American Christian Convention."

The North American Christian Convention was to do more than create an occasion and provide the platform for critical analyses of or bitter tirades against the International Convention and the United Society. It was to be marked by a positive rather than a negative emphasis; the wranglings associated with recent national gatherings had left a deep sense of dissatisfaction and a longing for something more edifying. There was a feeling of need on the part of those thoroughly committed to "the old paths" to walk in them again, to hold up the Scriptures as the divine and all-sufficient revelation of God and to emphasize the great doctrines of the Christian faith.

Convention Begins in 1927

About 3,500 gathered for the first "North American," which was held in Cadle Tabernacle, Indianapolis, October 12-16, 1927. Those who gathered for this convention were made more effective servants of Christ through the sharing of ideas relative to Christian service, were warmed by great fellowship, and were inspired by great preaching. Enthusiasm ran high. A continuation committee was selected to plan for another meeting the following year. With few exceptions, the North American Christian Convention has continued to meet each year. On occasion, registrations have been more than double the number at the first gathering. The North American has continued to be marked by selection of great themes, well-conceived and well-delivered messages showing depth of conviction and breadth of vision, and the same warm fellowship so in evidence at the first gathering, a fellowship in faith and in service.

BIBLE COLLEGES

The capture of American religious educational institutions by the liberal and critical school, including those founded by Disciples, could not fail to affect the Restoration movement, for the preachers were being educated in these institutions. The humanistic and rationalistic teaching, which made Christianity and its message of Christ primarily an ethical pattern rather than the redemptive program of God, was translated in varying degrees into the congregations in which these men served.

There was need for a rebirth of Biblical preaching, a re-emphasis upon the inspiration of the Bible, the deity of Jesus, and the

114

necessity and program for salvation from sin. This called for a new leadership having faith in and committed to these basic Christian doctrines. And the preparation of this new leadership called for new educational institutions. The answer to this need was the Bible college.

Colleges Established

Johnson Bible College, Kimberlin Heights, Tennessee, first known as "School of the Evangelists," was established by Ashley S. Johnson in 1893, and was an expression of the deep and abiding faith of its founder. Three more schools were organized during the first twenty years of the twentieth century: Minnesota Bible College, Kentucky Christian College, and Phillips Bible Institute (Canton, Ohio). (The latter school, although short-lived, contributed much to the movement.) The twenties saw three new schools: Cincinnati Bible Institute and McGarvey Bible College, merging after one year to form The Cincinnati Bible Seminary; Manhattan Bible College; and Pacific Bible Seminary, now Pacific Christian College. During the thirties Atlanta Christian College and San Jose Bible College came into existence.

The years 1940-1950 were fruitful Bible college years, producing Boise Bible College, Central Washington School of the Bible, Colegio Biblico, Dakota Bible College, Great Lakes Bible College, Intermountain Bible College, Lincoln Bible Institute, now Lincoln Christian College, Louisville Bible College, Midwest Christan College, Midwestern School of Evangelism, Nebraska Christian College, Ozark Bible College, Roanoke Bible College, Southern Christian College, Southwest Christian Seminary, Dallas Christian College, Puget Sound College of the Bible, and Mexican Bible Seminary.

The number of schools continued to grow during the next decade: Central Christian College of the Bible, Church of Christ School of Evangelism, Eastern Christian College, Grundy Bible Institute, Memphis Christian College, Platte Valley Bible College, St. Louis Christian College. In 1962 Paducah Christian College was begun.

Alberta Bible College is the oldest of the Canadian schools. Canada also has Toronto Christian Seminary and Maritime Christian College.

Two schools for training Negro workers have been established: College of the Scriptures and Winston-Salem Bible College.

Two graduate schools, the Graduate School of The Cincinnati

Bible Seminary, granting the B.D. degree, and Lincoln Christian Seminary of Lincoln Christian College, granting the M.A. and B.D. degrees, are maintained.

Curriculum and Growth

Bible colleges, designed to prepare workers for Christian service, have formed a curriculum of basic liberal arts, including courses in English, literature, science, logic, philosophy, world history, psychology, foreign language (Greek and Hebrew). In addition to these are the introductory, expository, and exegetical courses on the Bible, speech, homiletics, apologetics, hermeneutics, Christian doctrine, church history, Christian education, and music.

A liberal amount of criticism, some justified but much of it unjustified, has been leveled against the Bible college and its educational program. The name "glorified Sunday school" has been used in an attempt to ridicule the teaching program. Many schools have struggled for support, and some have died.

A number of the Bible colleges have taken on an educational stature comparable with that of other educational institutions in America in facilities, library, quality of teaching, and preparation of faculty. Several Bible colleges have been accredited by the Association of Bible Colleges, recognized agency for accrediting such institutions, and others are seeking accreditation. Academic hours earned in some of the Bible colleges have been accepted for transfer by schools accredited by other agencies, including state colleges and universities.

The Bible colleges have assets of more than thirteen and a half million dollars. The annual enrollment exceeds four thousand. A full-time faculty of over three hundred is maintained, supplemented by a part-time faculty of more than 150.

The contribution of the Bible colleges and justification for their teaching program, may be seen in the souls won to Christ, the closed churches opened, the weak churches strengthened, the new churches established, and the preachers, teachers, and missionaries now serving at home and abroad.

CHRISTIAN SERVICE CAMPS

Coming out of the same general background and conditions in the Restoration movement as direct-support missions and Bible colleges, and closely paralleling their rise and development, are the Christian service camps. Among the earliest developments were at Erieside (Ohio) and Lake James (Indiana). (A list of camps and

116

the weeks scheduled appears in *The Lookout* sometime in May or early June, and reports of the camps in a later issue.)

Christian service camps have had an almost unbelievable growth. In 1939 the number of students attending camps was about five thousand; in 1962 the number exceeded thirty-six thousand. The fifty weeks of camp provided in 1939 had grown to 458 weeks in the same period. A faculty of five thousand provides instruction and leadership.[3]

These camps provide instruction, inspiration, and recreation for Juniors, Junior High, and Senior High young people; some offer one or more weeks for adults. While primarily designed for Christian young people, a large number who are not Christians attend. Confessions and baptisms have averaged fifteen hundred or more in recent years.

The emphasis in these camps is upon Christian service in the local congregation or in wider areas. The challenge to commitment of life in specialized Christian service as preacher, teacher, missionary, director of music or Christian education, and church secretary has had over a thousand responses in some years and approximately this number in other years. At least ten camps have set up Life Recruit weeks in their camp schedules. From these life recruits have come many of the Bible college students.

Questions

1. What is meant by "direct-support" missions? How do such missions differ from other missionary programs?
2. What has led to the development and growth of direct-support missions?
3. What factors contributed to beginning the North American Christian Convention?
4. What gave rise to the Bible college movement? What is the basic purpose of the Bible college?
5. Name some of the Bible colleges.
6. What is a Christian service camp? What contribution do these camps make to the Restoration movement?

Notes

[1] Cf. *Millennial Harbinger*, 1850, pp. 282-287.
[2] *1963 Directory of the Ministry*. In 1962 Mr. Murch, *Christians Only*, p. 305, reports six hundred missionaries in eighteen lands.
[3] Cf. *1963 Directory of the Ministry*.

CHAPTER 13

Retrospect and Prospect

The Restoration movement is a Biblically-based and Christ-centered religious movement. It proposes that all Christians, and all who desire to become Christians, submit themselves completely to the Lord Jesus Christ, individually and collectively taking the New Testament as the standard for doctrine and conduct.

REFORMATION AND RESTORATION

The two words, "reformation" and "restoration," have been used indiscriminately in referring to this religious movement. Alexander Campbell, although continuing to use both words in referring to the movement, was careful to indicate its essential restorative character. In the first article of a series in the *Christian Baptist* entitled "A Restoration of the Ancient Order of Things," he wrote:

Since the New Testament was finished, it is fairly to be presumed that there cannot be any reformation of religion, properly so called. . . .

Human creeds may be reformed and re-reformed, and be erroneous still, like their authors; but the inspired creed needs no reformation, being, like its author, infallible. . . .

Human systems, whether of philosophy or of religion, are proper subjects of reformation; but christianity cannot be reformed. . . .

A restoration of the ancient order of things is all that is necessary to the happiness and usefulness of christians.[1]

The writer is certain that the following distinction has not been adhered to when using "reformation" and "restoration," but it is suggested as legitimate and proper when speaking about this movement. It is a "reformation" or "reformatory" movement when referring to the religious bodies, their creedal standards and ecclesiastical systems, to be affected; it is a "restoration" movement when referring to the divine standard by which changes are to be effected, the extent of the changes to be made, or the ultimate goals to be kept in sight. The "Restoration movement," then, is a movement designed to bring about a *complete* "reformation" or renovation of religion *according to the divine standard, the New Testament.*

118

RETROSPECT

When the Christian Association, and later the Brush Run Church, adopted the principle, "Where the Bible speaks, we speak; where the Bible is silent, we are silent," they committed themselves to a course which would lead to conflict with their religious neighbors. Obviously, the adoption of this slogan as the principle for reformatory action was indicative of a conviction that, in a large measure at least, the religious world was not speaking where the Bible speaks and was not silent where the Bible is silent.

Controversy Inevitable

Controversy was inevitable; for people, especially religious people, do not abandon practices or move out of well-established patterns of thought or action without great difficulty. Both offensive and defensive battles were fought. Occasions for condemning anti-Biblical practices and defenses against critical accusations brought by the established religious groups were frequent. Presbyterians, Baptists, Methodists, Universalists, Mormons, even a Roman Catholic, were met in public debate. A well-defined and extensive body of apologetic and polemic literature exists today as the fruit of these controversies.

Human Creeds Condemned

Human creeds were condemned as standards of faith and fellowship. They were opposed as being un-Scriptural, unnecessary, presumptuous, and factional. The "horrid evil" of a divided church, with its warring parties, was decried. Thomas Campbell, in the *Declaration and Address,* wrote of the "awful and distressing effects" of division: aversions, reproaches, backbitings, evil surmisings, angry contentions, enmities, excommunications, persecutions. A divided church did not rightly honor the Christ who was its head, ignoring His prayer for the unity of His followers as recorded in John 17; nor could it be an effective witness for Him in the world. Ecclesiastical systems, such as presbyteries, synods, general assemblies, and associations, holding disciplinary authority over the faith and conduct of individuals and churches, were considered anti-Scriptural and detrimental to the cause of Christ. But the movement was more than "anti-creed, anti-council, or anti-sectarian," as Alexander Campbell points out.[2] It is not just "anti," it is "pro"—pro-Bible, pro-Christ, pro-gospel, pro-union.

Much confusion and many errors had resulted from the failure to "rightly divide the word of truth," to differentiate between the dispensations covered in the Biblical record. Alexander Campbell's *Sermon on the Law*, which was an attempt to point out differences between the law and the gospel and to show the superiority of the latter, resulted in a "seven years' war" with the Baptists.

Doctrines of Calvinism Rejected

The basic doctrines of Calvinism—human inability, election, limited atonement, irresistibility of grace, and perseverance of the saints—were repudiated and rejected as unscriptural. Men were not to be considered puppets manipulated by God, or "totally depraved" creatures incapable of any good, but those whom God "so loved" and for whom Christ went to Calvary. The Calvinistic theology was charged with responsibility for the loss of countless numbers of souls who might have been saved by preaching the simple plan of salvation found in Acts. A sane evangelism, conforming to the pattern and examples found in the New Testament, was opposed to the emotional, "mourner's bench" type of conversion.

Movement Criticized

Much criticism was leveled against the message and the messengers of the movement. They were accused of bigotry, of claiming to be the only Christians; to which they replied, "We are not the only Christians, but we are Christians only." The practice of immersion "for the remission of sins" was proposed as evidence that these Christians believed in "baptismal regeneration" or "water salvation." The preaching of a *plan* of salvation—faith, repentance, confession, baptism, forgiveness of sin, gift of the Holy Spirit—which did not involve a period of anxiety and agonizing prayer, brought cries of "a heartless religion." The emphasis on man's ability to co-operate with God in his redemption was considered salvation by *works* and opposed to salvation by *grace*. And because they taught that the Holy Spirit operates through the Word in conversion rather than directly upon the sinner, they were accused of denying the Holy Spirit.

Name Discussed

The matter of the name to be worn was widely discussed in the formative period. Alexander Campbell urged the use of "Disciples" or "Disciples of Christ"; others—including Thomas Campbell, Walter Scott, and B. W. Stone—were convinced that "Christian Church" or "Church of Christ" was to be preferred as giving more honor to the Christ. While the latter names have been used to designate local congregations, those suggested by Alexander Campbell have been widely used to refer to the body of people.

Communion

Participation in the Communion was also discussed. Should Communion be open or closed? In particular, controversy centered in whether or not the unimmersed should be admitted. In their final decision most of the churches chose to make a different emphasis: Communion was neither open nor closed; no invitations were extended and no prohibitions announced. The individual rather than the corporate character of the Lord's Supper was stressed. No pre-Communion examinations were held to determine the fitness of communicants; there was no "policing" of those present at the hour of Communion. The Lord's table was prepared in the Lord's house each Lord's Day, and each individual present was called upon to consider the admonition of Paul: "Let a man examine himself, and so let him eat of that bread, and drink of that cup" (1 Corinthians 11:28).

Biblical Terminology Emphasized

An emphasis on using Biblical terminology led to the rejection of "Sabbath" when referring to the Lord's Day. "Trinity" was rejected because it was not found in the Bible. "Reverend" was not considered a proper title for preachers, since it is used only once in the Bible and then with reference to God (Psalm 111:9). Furthermore, since *all* believers are priests, there should be no division into "clergy" and "laity," no ministerial class to be set apart and designated as "reverends."

Slavery Issue

The controversy over slavery raged in a number of the prominent religious bodies, resulting in divisions into northern and southern bodies, each having its own standard and medium for co-operation. But while there was a strong anti-slavery sentiment, a sentiment sufficiently strong to lead to the organization of the Christian Missionary Society in which those opposed to slavery could conscientiously co-operate, no permanent division was created in Restoration forces. The position taken by Alexander Campbell played a prominent part in preventing division.

121

Legalism

Legalism marked the movement in some areas of thought and practice. The silences of the Scriptures were given a prohibitory character. Thomas Campbell's principle, designed to make a place for faith *and* opinion, in essence was rephrased to read: "Where the Bible speaks, we speak; where the Bible is silent, it speaks in prohibition." No room was left for opinion. The impact of this concept was manifested in the reaction to missionary societies and instrumental music in worship, which resulted in division among the churches.

Legalistic views further divided the Restoration movement, particularly the non-instrumental fellowship. The listing in Acts 2:42—apostles' teaching, fellowship, breaking of bread, prayers—was taken by some to be the divine *order* in worship, an order which would not be varied without violating New Testament teaching and incurring the wrath of God. Divergent views of the "lawfulness" of church buildings, orphan's homes, colleges for training preachers, divided classes for Bible study, use of lesson helps (such as quarterlies) brought divisions. Different concepts of the millennium were responsible for further severing fellowship.

An example of the extremes to which legalism has been pushed is found in two camps rising out of interpretations of the words of Jesus when He instituted the Memorial Supper, "He took the cup." Some hold that since Jesus took a *cup*, only a container having *handles* (which distinguishes a cup from a glass) may be used in the Communion. Others contend that Jesus took *the* cup, indicating that only *one* cup was used; therefore, more than one cup cannot be used.

Liberalism

Liberalism also has left its marks on the movement. Those adopting modern critical attitudes and methods of interpreting the Bible and its message gained sufficient influence to dominate the co-operative life of the movement, resulting in division into "liberals" and "conservatives" or "Co-operatives and Independents." The acceptance of the tenets of liberalism, although often covered over with other issues, has been the basic factor affecting the movement in the twentieth century. The influx of liberalism resulted in the development of the direct-support missionary program, Bible colleges, Christian service camps, the North American Christian Convention, and other conventions. These programs now display a remarkable vitality.

Movement Biblically-based

The Restoration movement was begun by men thoroughly convinced that the Bible was the Word of God, a unique book, divinely inspired and given to make known God's will to men. They were committed to understanding and preaching its message of redemption and oneness in Christ to an unsaved world and a divided church. Their plea was a Biblical plea, and it was, and is, valid only if the Scriptures are valid.

Modern critics may approach God's Word with a skeptical attitude, but these men approached it in reverent faith. Alexander Campbell dedicated the Christian Baptist "to all those, without distinction, who acknowledge the Scriptures of the Old and New Testaments to be a revelation from God; and the New Testament as containing the Religion of Jesus Christ:—who [are] willing to have all religious tenets and practices tried by the Divine Word."[3]

The normative character that Thomas Campbell conceived the Bible to have is seen throughout the *Declaration and Address*. In this historic document we have such expressions as: "conform to the model and accept the practice of the primitive church"; "the original pattern laid down in the New Testament"; "the divine Word is our standard"; "making a rule of it and *it alone*"; "what is expressly revealed and enjoined in the holy Scriptures." He characterized the Bible as "divinely revealed truths" and "legible and authentic records." Here was not just a rediscovery of the Bible; it was a re-emphasis upon its centrality and all-sufficiency in the Christian system.

The Bible, by charter, was included in the educational program at Bethany College. Alexander Campbell considered the place that he had assigned the Bible in the curriculum and teaching program made Bethany College unique among educational institutions of his day. Later schools made the same provision in their charters. A. S. Hayden, speaking of Western Reserve Eclectic Institute, indicated the high value placed upon the Bible by the founders of this institution:

The Bible is the foundation of all morality in the world. It contains all moral power for the improvement and refinement of the human race. Its counsels are eternal wisdom. Its morality is perfect. It cannot, therefore, be hazardous to lay the Bible as the moral basis of the Eclectic Institute.[4]

Movement Christ-centered

Christ is central in the Scriptures. He moves through the Word from the first promise of His coming in Genesis 3:15 to the close of Revelation. He is associated with the events of the first chapter of Genesis in the prologue of John's Gospel and the opening verses of Hebrews. Following the example of the apostolic messengers found in the Book of Acts, the preachers of the Restoration movement put Christ at the center of their preaching and activity.

According to Alexander Campbell, "the very soul, body, and spirit of the gospel—the marrow and fatness of Christianity—is in the proper answer to the question, *What think you of Christ? Who is He! What is He!*" And concerning the broader implications of the right concept of Christ he wrote, "Is not an agreement in the doctrine concerning Christ, or a *declaration of our faith in the person, mission, and character of Jesus Christ,* essential to Christian union—indeed, to an admission into any Christian community!"[5] Campbell refused union with Unitarians, who denied the deity of Jesus.

Walter Scott made the messiahship of Jesus the focal point of the entire Christian system. He wrote, "The proposition of the Mesiahship [sic] forms the basis or foundation of our religion." And again, "This is the master revelation, the *primum mobile* of the Christian Religion, the power that gives life and motion to all the other parts of the evangelical machinery. . . . Jesus is the Messiah the Son of God."[6]

PROSPECT

It has been said that the Restoration movement was born to die. And this is true . . . when its work is finished. Any movement that has lost its purpose or fulfilled its mission no longer has any reason for existence. But has the Restoration movement lost its purpose or fulfilled its mission? Do those factors which called it into being no longer exist?

Are there standards other than the Bible in Christianity today? In the early days human creeds were challenged as rightful standards for Christian conduct. While these historic symbols do not figure so prominently in the thinking of the "laity," they still continue to exist and to regulate religious bodies. Today, too, liberalism and humanism continue to challenge the Bible as a legitimate guide, suggesting that men follow the individual conscience or human experience. There is a trend, however, even among Biblical scholars, toward recognition of the validity of the Biblical record.

Is the church still divided? And is a divided church today any less a "horrid evil" than it was in 1809? A divided church fails to honor the Christ and fulfill His will as much today as it failed

124

in these respects yesterday. Today we hear much about unity: the ecumenical movement, the National Council of Churches, the World Council of Churches. The unity proposed, however, is not unity of Christians, it is the federation of denominations, the peaceful co-existence and collaboration in practical expression of Christianity. But, as Alexander Campbell observed in 1839, "The union of sects, and the union of Christians, are not identical propositions."[7]

Are there still unsaved men and women? Has the babel of voices directing sinners given place to the language of God? There are religious programs today as far from Biblical Christianity as those in the earliest days of the Restoration movement. Every sincere seeker after God has the right to and should be given, a clear, Biblical answer to the question, "What must I do to be saved?"

CONCLUSION

As a fitting conclusion to this study of the Restoration movement we propose the following evaluation by Alexander Campbell:

The ground assumed in the proposed reformation is the highest ground which can be assumed at any time or under any circumstances, and it is the only rational and lawful ground which human ingenuity and christian integrity can propose. . . . If we fail it cannot be in the object proposed: for in this no people can excel us—none can claim higher, more rational, or more scriptural ground. . . . If, too, christianity is ever to be restored . . . if the disciples of Jesus Christ are ever to be united, if sectarianism is ever to be put down, if the world is to be regenerated and its kingdoms to bow to the sceptre of Jesus . . . it must be by placing the Apostles upon the thrones which Jesus promised them, by making them the infallible arbiters of every question of faith and morals. . . If there be a rock, if there be a sure and well-tried foundation on which to build in the moral and religious desolations of christendom, this is the foundation.[8]

Questions

1. What is the difference between the concepts of "reformation" and "restoration" in religious matters?
2. What issues have been the cause of controversy between leaders of the Restoration movement and other religious groups?
3. What issues have been the cause of controversy within the Restoration movement?
4. Show how the Restoration movement is Biblically-based.
5. Show how the movement is Christ-centered.
6. Is there still need for the Restoration movement? Why?

Notes

[1] *Christian Baptist,* Burnet edition, pp. 127, 128.
[2] *Millennial Harbinger,* 1831, pp. 390, 391.
[3] *Christian Baptist,* Burnet edition, dedication page.
[4] Green, *Hiram College and Western Reserve Eclectic Institute,* p. 52.
[5] *Millennial Harbinger,* 1846, p. 222.
[6] *Gospel Restored,* pp. 131, 187.
[7] *Millennial Harbinger,* 1839, p. 344.
[8] *Ibid.,* 1831, pp. 417, 418.

SUGGESTED PROJECTS

1. Promote a church library or some other means whereby biographical, historical, and doctrinal books relating to the Restoration movement are made available for reading to the congregation.
2. Gather, or help in collecting, materials for a history of your congregation.
3. Promote the writing of this history in conjunction with the minister and others in the congregation who are interested.
4. If possible, make available interesting historical and doctrinal information for the church bulletin or paper.
5. Have a church historian appointed or elected who will be responsible for direction in the collecting and preservation of historical materials such as the following:
   a) Pictures—preachers, missionaries, church groups, classes, buildings, etc.
   b) Local church papers, weekly bulletins, etc.
   c) A scrapbook from local newspapers and religious journals concerning the church, its organizations, its ministry, activities, members. Be sure to indicate date, title of article, and name of paper in each instance.
6. Perhaps the congregation would be interested in a campaign to obtain subscribers for a religious periodical related to the Restoration movement, such as the *Christian Standard.*
7. Plan some special services relating to the movement, such as a hymn service in which the writers and hymns of those associated with the Restoration movement might be featured.
8. Keep a missionary file or scrapbook.
9. Keep a Bible college file of a number of Bible colleges.
10. At some suitable time, have a report on some interesting volume of Restoration movement literature, such as *The Fool of God* (Cochran), *Raccoon John Smith* (Cochran), or *"P.H." the Welshimer Story* (Arant).
11. Have someone review one of the early documents.

BIBLIOGRAPHY

Books

BAXTER, WILLIAM. *Life of Elder Walter Scott.* Cincinnati: Bosworth, Chase and Hall, 1874.

CAMPBELL, ALEXANDER. *The Christian System.* Cincinnati: Standard Publishing Company, 1835.

————. *Memoirs of Elder Thomas Campbell.* Cincinnati: H. S. Bosworth, 1861.

COCHRAN, LOUIS. *Raccoon John Smith.* New York: Duell, Sloan, and Pearce, 1963.

————. *The Fool of God.* New York: Duell, Sloan, and Pearce, 1958.

COREY, S. J. *Fifty Years of Attack and Controversy.* Des Moines: Committee on Publication of the Corey Manuscript, 1953.

Directory of the Ministry. Springfield, Illinois: Directory of the Ministry, 1963.

EVANS, MADISON. *Biographical Sketches of the Pioneer Preachers of Indiana.* Philadelphia: J. Challen & Sons, 1862.

GARRISON, W. E., and DEGROOT, A. T. *The Disciples of Christ: A History.* St. Louis: Christian Board of Publication, 1948.

GATES, ERRETT. *Early Relation and Separation of Baptists and Disciples.* Chicago: Christian Century Company, 1904.

GREEN, F. M. *Hiram College and Western Reserve Eclectic Institute.* Cleveland: O. S. Hubbell Printing Company, 1901.

HALEY, J. J. *Debates That Made History.* St. Louis: Christian Board of Publication, 1920.

HANNA, W. H. *Thomas Campbell, Seceder and Christian Union Advocate.* Cincinnati: Standard Publishing Company, 1935.

HAYDEN, A. S. *Early History of the Disciples in the Western Reserve.* Cincinnati: Chase & Hall, 1875.

HAYDEN, EDWIN V. *Fifty Years of Digression and Disturbance.* Joplin, Missouri: Hunter Printing Co., n. d.

JENNINGS, W. W. *Origin and Early History of the Disciples of Christ.* Cincinnati: Standard Publishing Company, 1919.

KERSHNER, F. D., and PHILLIPS, WOODROW. *The Restoration Handbook.* Five series. San Antonio: Southern Christian Press, 1960.

LAMAR, J. S. *Memoirs of Isaac Errett.* Vol. I. Cincinnati: Standard Publishing Company, 1893.

Lewis, Grant K. *The American Christian Missionary Society*. St. Louis: Christian Board of Publication, 1937.

MacClenny, W. E. *The Life of Rev. James O'Kelly*. Indianapolis: Religious Book Service, 1950 (reprint).

Moore, W. T. *A Comprehensive History of the Disciples of Christ*. New York: Fleming H. Revell, 1909.

Morrill, M. T. *A History of the Christian Denomination in America*. Dayton, Ohio: Christian Publishing Association, 1912.

Murch, James De Forest. *Christians Only*. Cincinnati: Standard Publishing Company, 1962.

Richardson, R. *Memoirs of Alexander Campbell*. 2 vol. in one. Cincinnati: Standard Publishing Company, n.d.

Rogers, John. *The Biography of Elder Barton Warren Stone*. Cincinnati: J. A. & U. P. James, 1847.

Scott, Walter. *The Gospel Restored*. Cincinnati: O. H. Donogh, 1836.

Ware, C. C. *Barton Warren Stone*. St. Louis: Bethany Press, 1932.

Welshimer, P. H. *Concerning the Disciples*. Cincinnati: Standard Publishing Company, 1935.

Williams, J. A. *Life of Elder John Smith*. Cincinnati: R. W. Carroll & Company, 1870.

Witmer, S. A. *The Bible College: Education With Dimension*. Manhasset, New York: Channel Press, 1962.

Young, C. A. *Historical Documents Advocating Christian Union*. Chicago: Christian Century Company, 1904.

Periodicals

Christian Baptist, 1823-1830. Alexander Campbell, ed.
Christian Messenger, 1826-1845. Barton W. Stone, ed.
Millennial Harbinger, 1830-1870. Alexander Campbell, ed.